英和対訳

ケネディ大統領演説集

Major Speeches of President John F. Kennedy

訳注
長谷川 潔

南雲堂

はしがき

　アメリカの歴代の大統領のうち，リンカーンとケネディがもっともすぐれた演説家であるという。

　アメリカ第35代の大統領ジョン・F・ケネディは，1961年1月20日に就任し，1963年11月22日テキサス州で悲劇的な死をとげました。

　アメリカ屈指の雄弁家として知られた故ケネディ大統領が残した数多くの演説のうちから，特に代表的なものを選び，日・英対訳にして本書に収めました。

　故ケネディ大統領の生前，彼の演説を批評して，ニューヨーク・タイムズ紙は次のようにのべていました。

「ジョン・F・ケネディはホワイトハウスを去る前に，米国史上もっとも有名な演説家になっているであろう」

　たしかに，

「国が自分に何をしてくれるかを問い給うな。自分が国に何ができるかを問い給え」

"Ask not what your country can do for you——ask what you can do for your country."

「恐れから交渉をすることはやめましょう。しかし，交渉することは恐れないでやりましょう」

"Let us never negotiate out of fear. But let us never fear to negotiate."

　などの名文句にいろどられた彼の就任演説（1961年1月20日）は，すでにリンカーン，ウィルソン，フランクリン・D・ルーズベルトなどの演説にも匹敵する名演説だと

いわれています。ピューリツァー賞受賞者である彼の文才をしのばせる多くの演説は，その簡潔な表現と格調の高さにおいて，現代英語の最もすぐれた散文の一つとしても評価されています。

「偉大な人間の場合，彼について論じたものよりも，彼自身が語ったことの方がはるかに価値がある」という言葉は，ケネディ大統領についてもぴたりとあてはまります。この意味で，崇高な理想に燃えて世界平和から黒人問題にいたるまでを追求した彼の演説は，わが国の若い人たちの間に強い共感を呼びおこしてきました。

　故ケネディ大統領の演説集は，彼の死後半年たらずの1964年4月に，南雲堂より英文テキストとして出版され，毎年多くの人々に読みつがれ，現在，50数刷にも達しています。

　彼の死後20年余の間に，ジョンソン，ニクソン，フォード，カーター，レーガンなどのアメリカ大統領が次々とすぐれた演説を行なっています。しかし，ケネディの演説ほど息長く多くの人々の記憶の中に残っている名演説は出ていません。英文テキストとして，アメリカ，日本をはじめ，世界の国々で読みつがれているアメリカ大統領の演説は，リンカーンのゲティスバークの演説と共に，ケネディ大統領の演説がもっとも人気があると言われています。

　考える人，行動する人として，人類のために世界の平和を訴え続けた彼の演説は，20年以上たった現在でも，私たちの心を強くゆり動かし続けています。だからこそ，高校や大学をはじめ，職場の英語クラブで行われる朗唱大会で，上述した彼の演説の一節が，日本の若い人たちの口からほ

とばしり出てくるのではないでしょうか。

　今回，訳をつけて英文の対訳としたのは，歴史的な彼の演説をさらに多くの人々に深く理解していただき，平和の戦略に対するわれわれ日本人の態度を再検討していただきたいからにほかなりません。

　本書の最後につけ加えた「続けようではないか」の演説は，ジョンソン第36代大統領が，故ケネディ大統領の残した業績を引きついでいく決意を明らかにしたものです。

　今回の対訳にあたっては，アメリカ大使館文化交換局出版部発行の資料・パンフレットなどを全面的に参考にしました。資料提供の便宜を与えられ，その使用を快諾された，同大使館出版部のご厚意に深く感謝いたします。また，演説の録音テープの入手と使用については，同じアメリカ大使館ラジオ部のお世話になりました。

　なお，参考資料の整理，原文と対訳分との対照チェックや原稿の清書などについては，大東文化大学の小池直己専任講師と駿河台予備校の片山七三雄講師にお願いしました。ここに感謝のことばと共に心からお礼を申し上げます。

長 谷 川　潔

Disk 1―色つきの個所でケネディ大統領とジョンソン
　　　　大統領の生の音声CD
Disk 2―スタジオ録音による別音声のCD

も　く　じ

はしがき ……………………………………………… iii

ケネディ大統領の就任演説 ……………………… 2
　PRESIDENT KENNEDY'S
　INAUGURAL ADDRESS

平和の戦略 …………………………………………14
　THE STRATEGY OF PEACE

核実験停止条約に関する演説 ……………………42
　BANNING NUCLEAR TESTS

平和の建設 …………………………………………70
　BUILDING THE PEACE

続けようではありませんか ………………………104
　WE WILL CARRY ON

NOTES ………………………………………………121

録音CDについて …………………………………132

ケネディ大統領演説集

PRESIDENT KENNEDY'S INAUGURAL ADDRESS

Fellow Citizens:

We observe today not a victory of party but a celebration of freedom—symbolizing an end as well as a beginning—signifying renewal as well as change. For I have sworn before you and Almighty God the same solemn oath our forebears prescribed nearly a century and three quarters ago.

The world is very different now. For man holds in his mortal hands the power to abolish all forms of human poverty and all forms of human life. And yet the same revolutionary beliefs for which our forebears fought are still at issue around the globe—the belief that the rights of man come not from the generosity of the state but from the hand of God.

We dare not forget today that we are the heirs of that first revolution. Let the word go forth from this time and place, to friend and foe alike, that the torch has been passed to a new generation of Americans—born in this century, tempered by war, disciplined by a hard and bitter peace, proud of our ancient

ケネディ大統領の就任演説

　市民諸君，

　われわれは，今日，党の勝利を祝っているのではなくて，自由の祭典――始まりとともに終りを象徴し，変革とともに更新を意味する――を祝っているのであります。なぜならば私は，いま，われわれの祖先が175年近くも昔に定めたものと同じ厳粛な誓いを諸君と全能の神の前で誓ったからであります。

　世界は今日非常に変わりました。なぜなら，人類はあらゆる形の人間の貧困とあらゆる形の人間の生活を廃絶させうる力をその手に握っているからであります。しかも，われわれの祖先が擁護すべく闘った同じ革命的な信念――人間の諸権利は国家の寛容からくるのではなく，神の手からくるのであるという信念――は今日依然として世界中で争点になっているのです。

　われわれは今日，われわれがかの最初の革命の継承者であることを決して忘れるものではありません。今この時，この場所から，友に対しても敵に対しても一様に次の言葉を伝えようではありませんか――たいまつは新しい世代の米国民に引き継がれた――それはこの世紀に生まれ，戦争によって鍛えられ，厳しい平和によって訓練され，われわれの古い遺産

heritage—and unwilling to witness or permit the slow undoing of those human rights to which this nation has always been committed, and to which we are committed today at home and around the world.

Let every nation know, whether it wishes us well or ill, that we shall pay any price, bear any burden, meet any hardship, support any friend, oppose any foe to assure the survival and the success of liberty.

This much we pledge—and more.

To those old allies whose cultural and spiritual origins we share, we pledge the loyalty of faithful friends. United, there is little we cannot do in a host of cooperative ventures. Divided, there is little we can do—for we dare not meet a powerful challenge at odds and split asunder.

To those new states whom we welcome to the ranks of the free, we pledge our word that one form of colonial control shall not have passed away merely to be replaced by a far more iron tyranny. We shall not always expect to find them supporting our view. But we shall always hope to find them strongly supporting their own freedom—and to remember that, in the past, those who foolishly sought power by riding the back of the tiger ended up inside.

To those people in the huts and villages of half the globe struggling to break the bonds of mass misery, we pledge our best efforts to help them help

を誇りとし，この国がつねに擁護することを誓ってきた諸々の人権，そして，今日われわれが国内ならびに世界において擁護することを誓っている諸々の人権がしだいに葬り去られるのを目撃し，もしくは容認することをいさぎよしとしない新しい世代の米国民であります。

　われわれに好意をもつ国と悪意をもつ国を問わず，あらゆる国をして，自由の存続と成功を確保するためには，われわれはいかなる代価をも支払い，いかなる重荷をもにない，いかなる苦難にも立ち向かい，いかなる友をも支援し，いかなる敵にも対抗するものであることを知らしめよう。

　これだけのことをわれわれは誓う——そして，さらに多くのことを。

　文化的，精神的起源をひとしくする古くからの盟友に対して，われわれは忠実な友としての忠誠を誓うものであります。われわれが結束する時，多くの共同事業においてなしえないことはほとんどありません。しかし，分裂するとき，われわれはほとんど何事もなしえないのです——なぜならば，互いに争い，ばらばらに分裂したままでは，とうてい強力な挑戦に応じることはできないからであります。

　われわれが自由世界の仲間に迎えつつある新興諸国に対しては，一つの型の植民地支配が過ぎ去ったあとに，単にそれよりもはるかに冷酷な専制がとって代わるというようなことは断じてさせないということをわれわれは誓います。われわれはこれらの国がわれわれの見解を支持することをつねに期待するものではありません。しかしわれわれは彼らが彼ら自身の自由を強く支持する姿をみたいとつねに希望し，また過去において愚かにも虎にまたがって権力をえようとしたものが，結局虎にくわれてしまったということを思いおこすよう，つねに希望するものであります。

　地球の半分にわたって存在するあばら屋や村落に住み，集団的な悲惨の鎖を断ち切ろうとして苦闘している人々に対して，われわれはその必要がつづくかぎりいつまでも，彼らの

themselves, for whatever period is required—not because the communists may be doing it, not because we seek their votes, but because it is right. If a free society cannot help the many who are poor, it cannot save the few who are rich.

To our sister republics south of our border, we offer a special pledge—to convert our good words into good deeds—in a new alliance for progress—to assist free men and free governments in casting off the chains of poverty. But this peaceful revolution of hope cannot become the prey of hostile powers. Let all our neighbors know that we shall join with them to oppose aggression or subversion anywhere in the Americas. And let every other power know that this hemisphere intends to remain the master of its own house.

To that world assembly of sovereign states, the United Nations, our last best hope in an age where the instruments of war have far outpaced the instruments of peace, we renew our pledge of support—to prevent it becoming merely a forum for invective—to strengthen its shield of the new and the weak —and to enlarge the area in which its writ may run.

Finally, to those nations who would make themselves our adversary, we offer not a pledge but a request: that both sides begin anew the quest for peace, before the dark powers of destruction unleashed

自立を助けるために全力をつくすことを誓う——それは共産主義者がそうしているかも知れないからではなく，また彼らの投票をわれわれが求めるからではなく，そうすることが正しいからです。もし自由社会が貧しい多くの人々を助けることができないならば，富める少数の人々を救うこともできないのです。

われわれの国境の南方にある姉妹共和国に対して，われわれは——われわれの善い言葉を善い行ないに移し——進歩のための新しい提携によって自由な国民や自由な政府が貧困の鎖を払いのけるのを助けるとの特別の約束をします。しかし，この平和的希望の革命が敵意をもつ諸国のえじきになるようなことがあってはならないのです。すべてのわが近隣諸国には，われわれは互いに手をたずさえて，米州内のいかなる国に対する侵略や破壊工作にも対抗するものであることを知ってもらいたいのです。また米州があくまで自家の主人でありたいと考えていることを，他のいずれの国にも知ってもらいたいのです。

主権国家の世界会議である国際連合，戦争の手段を遠く追い越してしまった時代のわれわれの最後の，そして最大の希望である国際連合に対して，それが単に中傷のやりとりの場にすぎないものになることを防ぎ，新しい国，弱い国を守る国連の力を強め，国連憲章のおよぶ地域をおしひろげるよう，われわれは支持の誓いを新たにするものであります。

最後に，われわれの敵対者になろうとしている国々に対して，われわれは誓約ではなく，要求を提出する——科学によって解放された暗黒の破壊力が，計画的にもしくは偶発的に

by science engulf all humanity in planned or accidental self-destruction.

We dare not tempt them with weakness. For only when our arms are sufficient beyond doubt can we be ⁵certain beyond doubt that they will never be employed.

But neither can two great and powerful groups of nations take comfort from our present course—both sides overburdened by the cost of modern weapons, both rightly alarmed by the steady spread of the ¹⁰deadly atom, yet both racing to alter that uncertain balance of terror that stays the hand of mankind's final war.

So let us begin anew—remembering on both sides that civility is not a sign of weakness, and sincerity ¹⁵is always subject to proof. Let us never negotiate out of fear. But let us never fear to negotiate.

Let both sides explore what problems unite us instead of belaboring those problems which divide us.

Let both sides, for the first time, formulate serious ²⁰and precise proposals for the inspection and control of arms—and bring the absolute power to destroy other nations under the absolute control of all nations.

Let both sides seek to invoke the wonders of science instead of its terrors. Together let us explore the ²⁵stars, conquer the deserts, eradicate disease, tap the ocean depths, and encourage the arts and commerce.

Let both sides unite to heed in all corners of the

全人類を自己破滅におとしいれる前に，両者で新しく平和への探求を始めようではありませんか。
　われわれは弱みをみせて，相手に手を出させるような誘惑を決して与えません。なぜならば，武力が疑いの余地なく十分な場合にのみ，武力は疑いの余地なく用いられないと確信するからであります。
　しかし，また二つの大きな強力な国家群はそれぞれの現在の進路から慰めを得ることはできない——双方とも近代兵器のコストによって過度の負担を負わされ，双方とも恐ろしい原子の着実な拡大にまさしく恐怖を感じながら，しかも人類の最終戦をくいとめている，あの不安定な恐怖の均衡を変えようと競争をつづけているからです。
　そこで，われわれは，双方の側とも，丁重さは弱さを示すものではなく，誠実さはつねに証明されなければならないということを思いおこしながら，改めて出直そうではありませんか。われわれは決して恐怖心から交渉してはなりません。しかし，交渉することを決して恐れてはならないのです。双方ともわれわれを分裂させている諸問題に力を注ぐかわりに，われわれを結びつける一切の問題を探求しようではありませんか。
　双方とも，まず第一に軍備の査察と規制のためのまじめで，精密な提案を作り——そして，他の諸国を破壊する絶対的な力を，すべての国々の絶対的な管理のもとにおこうではありませんか。
　双方とも，科学の恐怖ではなしに科学の驚異をひき出すために力を合わせようではないですか。われわれは協力して天体を探査し，砂漠を征服し，病気を根絶し，深海を開発し，学芸と通商を奨励しようではありませんか。
　双方とも，「くびきのひもをとき……しいたげられる者を

earth the command of Isaiah—to "undo the heavy burdens ... and let the oppressed go free."

And if a beachhead of cooperation may push back the jungle of suspicion, let both sides join in creating a new endeavor, not a new balance of power, but a new world of law, where the strong are just and the weak secure, and the peace preserved.

All this will not be finished in the first one hundred days. Nor will it be finished in the first one thousand days, nor in the life of this administration, nor even perhaps in our lifetime on this planet. But let us begin.

In your hands, my fellow citizens, more than mine, will rest the final success or failure of our course. Since this country was founded, each generation of Americans has been summoned to give testimony to its national loyalty. The graves of young Americans who answered the call to service surround the globe.

Now the trumpet summons us again—not as a call to bear arms, though arms we need—not as a call to battle, though embattled we are—but a call to bear the burden of a long twilight struggle, year in and year out, "rejoicing in hope, patient in tribulation" —a struggle against the common enemies of man: tyranny, poverty, disease and war itself.

Can we forge against these enemies a grand and global alliance, North and South, East and West, that

放ち去らせ」というイザヤのことばを地球上のあらゆる隅々の人々の心に留めさせるために，力を合わせようではありませんか。

そして，もし協力の拠点が嫌疑のジャングルを押し返すことができたならば，双方とも新しい創造の試み，すなわち新しい力の均衡ではなく，強者は公正であり，弱者は安全であり，平和が保たれる新しい法の世界を創り出すことに全力を合わせようではありませんか。

これらすべてのことは，最初の100日間で成し遂げられるものではありません。また最初の1000日間，さらにはこの政権の任期中，あるいはこの地球上において，われわれが生きている間にはおそらく成し遂げられないでしょう。でも，始めようではないですか。

われわれの方針が究極的に成功するか失敗するかは，私の肩以上に市民諸君，諸君の肩にかかっているのです。この国の建国以来，米国民の各世代は国家に対するその忠誠を立証することを要請されてきました。軍務につけとの召集に答えた若い米国民の墓標は地球をとりまいております。

いまや召集のラッパが再びわれわれを呼んでいます——それは武器をとれとの呼びかけではありません。もっとも武器は必要ではありますが，それは戦闘への呼びかけでもありません，われわれは抗争してはいますが——それは来る年，行く年，「望みをいだいて喜び，艱難に耐え」る長い夜明け前の闘争——専制，貧困，病気，戦争そのものといった，人類の共通の敵に対する闘争という重荷をになえとの呼びかけであります。

これらの敵に対して，われわれは全人類による実り多い生活を保証しうる東と西，南と北をふくめた世界的大同盟を形

can assure a more fruitful life for all mankind? Will you join in that historic effort?

In the long history of the world, only a few generations have been granted the role of defending freedom in its hour of maximum danger. I do not shrink from this responsibility—I welcome it. I do not believe that any of us would exchange places with any other people or any other generation. The energy, the faith, the devotion which we bring to this endeavor will light our country and all who serve it—and the glow from that fire can truly light the world.

And so, my fellow Americans: ask not what your country can do for you—ask what you can do for your country.

My fellow citizens of the world: ask not what America will do for you, but what together we can do for the freedom of man.

Finally, whether you are citizens of America or citizens of the world, ask of us here the same high standards of strength and sacrifice which we ask of you. With a good conscience our only sure reward, with history the final judge of our deeds, let us go forth to lead the land we love, asking His blessing and His help, but knowing that here on earth, God's work must truly be our own.

成することができるではありませんか。この歴史的な努力に参加していただけるでありましょうか。

　世界の長い歴史のなかで，自由の最大の危機のときに，自由を守る役割を授けられた世代はごく少ないのです。私はこの責任からしりごみしません。私はそれを歓迎いたします。この地位を他の国民，他の世代と取り替えたいと思っているものは，われわれの中にただの一人もいないと私は確信します。こうした努力に向けるわれわれの精力，信念，献身こそ，わが国とそれに仕えるすべての人々を照らし，――またその火から発する光は本当に世界を照らすことができるのであります。

　それゆえ，わが同胞であるアメリカ人諸君，諸君の国が諸君のために何をなしうるかを問い給うな――諸君が諸君の国のために何をなしうるかを問い給え。

　わが友である世界の市民諸君，米国が諸君のために何をなすかを問い給うな。人類の自由のために，われわれが共に何をなしうるかを問い給え。

　最後に，諸君が米国市民であろうと，世界の市民であろうと，われわれが諸君に求めるのと同じくらい高い水準の力と犠牲をわれわれに求め給え。安らかな良心をわれわれの唯一のたしかな報酬とし，歴史をもってわれわれの行ないの究極の審判となし，神の恵みと助けを求めるが，この地上では神の御業が真にわれわれ自身の所業でなければならないということをわきまえながら，わが愛する国土を導いて前進しようではありませんか。

THE STRATEGY OF PEACE

"There are few earthly things more beautiful than a university," wrote John Masefield, in his tribute to the English universities—and his words are equally true here. He did not refer to spires and towers, to campus greens and ivied walls. He admired the splendid beauty of the university, he said, because it was "a place where those who hate ignorance may strive to know, where those who perceive truth may strive to make others see."

I have, therefore, chosen this time and this place to discuss a topic on which ignorance too often abounds and the truth is too rarely perceived—yet it is the most important topic on earth: world peace.

What kind of peace do I mean? What kind of peace do we seek? Not a Pax Americana enforced on the world by American weapons of war. Not the peace of the grave or the security of the slave. I am talking about genuine peace—the kind of peace that makes life on earth worth living—the kind that enables men and nations to grow and hope and to build a better life for their children—not merely peace for Americans but peace for all mankind—not merely

平　和　の　戦　略

「この地上にあるもので，大学ほど美しいものはあまりない」とジョン・メイスフィールドはイギリスの大学の賛辞のなかで述べています。そして，この言葉はこの大学についても同様に当てはまります。彼はとがった屋根や塔，学園の芝生やツタの生い茂った壁のことを指して言ったのではないのです。彼が大学のすばらしい美しさを称賛したのは，大学が「無知を憎む人々が真理を知ろうと努力し，真理を知っている人が，他の人々の目を開かせようと努力する場所」だからです。

それゆえ，私は，無知があまりにもはびこり，真実がまれにしか理解されていない問題ではありながら，地上で最も重要な問題である世界平和について述べるために，この時とこの場所を選んだのです。

どのような平和を私は心に描いているのでしょうか。どのような平和をわれわれは求めているのでありましょうか。それは決してアメリカの兵器によって世界に押しつけられる「パックス・アメリカーナ」（米国が強制する平和）ではありません。それは，墓場の平和でも，奴隷の安全でもないのです。私は本当の平和，すなわち，地上の生活を生きがいあるものにするような平和，人と国が成長し，希望をもち，子孫のためによりよい生活を築くことが出来るような平和，単に米国人のための平和ではなく，全人類のための平和，単にわ

peace in our time but peace for all time.

I speak of peace because of the new face of war. Total war makes no sense in an age when great powers can maintain large and relatively invulnerable nuclear forces and refuse to surrender without resort to those forces. It makes no sense in an age when a single nuclear weapon contains almost ten times the explosive force delivered by all of the Allied air forces in the Second World War. It makes no sense in an age when the deadly poisons produced by a nuclear exchange would be carried by wind and water and soil and seed to the far corners of the globe and to generations unborn.

Today, the expenditure of billions of dollars every year on weapons acquired for the purpose of making sure we never need to use them is essential to keeping the peace. But surely the acquisition of such idle stockpiles—which can only destroy and can never create—is not the only, much less the most efficient, means of assuring peace.

I speak of peace, therefore, as the necessary rational end of rational men. I realize that the pursuit of peace is not as dramatic as the pursuit of war—and frequently the words of the pursuer fall on weary ears. But we have no more urgent task.

Some say that it is useless to speak of world peace or world law or world disarmament—and that it will

れわれの時代だけの平和ではなく，永遠の平和について語ってゆくつもりです。

　戦争の新しい様相ゆえに，私はまず平和について語りたいと思います。全面戦争は大国が大きな，比較的破壊しにくい核戦力を保持し，そうした戦力に訴えないかぎり降伏することを拒めるような時代には，無意味であります。たった一個の核兵器が，第二次世界大戦で，連合国側の空軍全部が投下した爆弾の十倍近い威力を持っている時代には，全面戦争は無意味であります。また，核交戦によって生み出される毒物が，風，水，土，種子によって，地球のすみずみにまで運ばれ，まだ生まれていない世代にまで影響を与えるような時代には，全面戦争は無意味であります。

　今日，われわれがそれを使う必要性をなくすために調達されている兵器に対して，毎年費やされている何十億ドルもの支出は，平和を維持するために絶対に必要なのです。しかし，破壊することができるだけで，決して創造することができない，こうした遊休兵器の蓄積が，平和確保の唯一の方法ではなく，いわんや最も有効な方法でないことは確かであります。

　それゆえ私は，理性的な人々が必然的にもつべき合理的目的としての平和について語っているのであります。私は，平和の追求が戦争の追求ほど劇的でないことを知っております。そしてしばしば平和追求者の言葉は，またかというように聞き流されてしまいます。しかし，これ以上緊急を要する仕事はないのです。

　世界平和，世界法あるいは世界の軍備撤廃について語ることは無益である，ソ連の指導者がもっと，もののわかった態

be useless until the leaders of the Soviet Union adopt a more enlightened attitude. I hope they do. I believe we can help them to do it. But I also believe that we must re-examine our own attitude—as individuals and as a nation—for our attitude is as essential as theirs. And every graduate of this school, every thoughtful citizen who despairs of war and wishes to help bring peace, should begin by looking inward—by examining his own attitude toward the possibilities of peace, toward the Soviet Union, toward the course of the Cold War, and toward freedom and peace here at home.

First: let us re-examine our attitude toward peace itself. Too many of us think it impossible. Too many think it unreal. But that is a dangerous, defeatist belief. It leads to the conclusion that war is inevitable—that mankind is doomed—that we are gripped by forces we cannot control.

We need not accept that view. Our problems are man-made—therefore, they can be solved by man. And man can be as big as he wants. No problem of human destiny is beyond the reach of human beings. Man's reason and spirit have often solved the seemingly unsolvable—and we believe they can do it again.

I am not referring to the absolute, infinite concept of universal peace and good will of which some fan-

度をとるようになるまでは無益である，という人々が一部におります。私はソ連の人々がそうした態度をとることを希望しております。われわれは彼らがそうするのを助けることが出来ると信じているのです。しかし，同時に私は，われわれも個人として，国家として，われわれ自身の態度を再検討しなければならないと信じております。われわれの態度は彼らの態度と同じくらい重要だからです。そしてこの大学のあらゆる卒業生，戦争に絶望し，平和をもたらすことに助力したいと願っているあらゆる思慮ある市民は，まず内へ目を向けて，平和の可能性に対する，ソ連に対する，冷戦の経過に対する，また米国内の自由と平和に対する，自分自身の態度を検討しはじめるべきであります。

　まず第一に，平和自体に対するわれわれの態度を再検討してみましょう。あまりに多くの人々が平和は不可能である，非現実的であると考えていますが，これは危険な，敗北主義的な考え方です。それは戦争は不可避である，人類は破滅の運命にある，われわれは支配することの出来ない力によって支配されている，という結論に達します。しかし，われわれは，こうした考えを受け入れる必要はありません。われわれの問題は人間が生んだものなのです。それゆえ，人間はそれを解決することが出来ます。そして人間は自分が望むだけ大きくなれるものです。人間の運命に関するどんな問題も，人間の力の範囲外のものはないのです。人間の理性と精神は，これまでにもしばしば一見，解決不可能な問題を解決してきました。われわれは人間がこの問題を解決することが出来ると信じています。

　私は，一部の空想家や狂信者がいまなお夢みている全世界の平和や善意といった絶対的，無限の概念のことをいってい

tasies and fanatics still dream. I do not deny the values of hopes and dreams, but we would merely invite discouragement and incredulity by making that our only and immediate goal.

Let us focus instead on a more practical, more attainable peace—based not on a sudden revolution in human nature but on a gradual evolution in human institutions—on a series of concrete actions and effective agreements which are in the interest of all concerned. There is no single, simple key to this peace —no grand or magic formula to be adopted by one or two powers. Genuine peace must be the product of many nations, the sum of many acts. It must be dynamic, not static, changing to meet the challenge of each generation. For peace is a process—a way of solving problems.

With such a peace, there will still be quarrels and conflicting interests, as there are within families and nations. World peace, like community peace, does not require that each man love his neighbor—it requires only that they live together with mutual tolerance, submitting their disputes to a just and peaceful settlement. And history teaches us that enmities between nations, as between individuals, do not last forever. However fixed our likes and dislikes may seem, the tide of time and events will often bring surprising shifts in the relations between nations and

るのではありません。私は希望や夢の価値を否定しませんが，これらをわれわれの当面の，唯一の目標にしたならば，いたずらに失望と懐疑を招くだけであると思います。

そうでなくて，より実際的な，達成可能な平和，すなわち，人間性の急激な革命ではなくて，人間のもろもろの制度の漸進的進化に基づいて，関係者すべての利益になる一連の具体的措置と有効な協定に基づく，平和に力を注ごうではありませんか。こうした平和を切り開くための一個で間に合うような簡単なカギはありませんし，また，一つや二つの国の勢力によって採択された魔力をもった一大方式などというものもないのです。真の平和は多くの国々の協力によって，生み出されたものでなければならないし，それは，多くの一措置が重なって初めて作り出されるものなのです。それは静的なものでなく，動的で，各時代の挑戦に応じて，変化するものでなければならないのです。なぜならば平和とは一つの過程であり，問題を解決するための一つの方法であるからです。

たとえこうした平和が存在したとしても，家族の内部におけるのと同じように，依然として争いや利害の対立が残るでしょう。世界の平和は，地域社会の平和と同じく，各人が隣人を愛することを要求せず，ただ単に彼らが互いに寛容の心をもって共存し，その紛争を公正で平和的な解決方法に委ねることを要求するものです。そして歴史は，諸国間の敵対関係が，個人の場合と同じように，永久に続くものではないことを，われわれに教えてくれています。われわれの好ききらいがどんなに固定したものにみえたとしても，時代と事態の潮流は，しばしば国家間，隣人間の関係に驚くべき変化をも

neighbors.

So let us persevere. Peace need not be impracticable—and war need not be inevitable. By defining our goal more clearly—by making it seem more manageable and less remote—we can help all peoples to see it, to draw hope from it, and to move irresistibly toward it.

Second: let us re-examine our attitude toward the Soviet Union. It is discouraging to think that their leaders may actually believe what their propagandists continually write. It is discouraging to read a recent authoritative Soviet text on military strategy and find, on page after page, wholly baseless and incredible claims—such as the allegation that "American imperialist circles are preparing to unleash different types of wars ... that there is a very real threat of a preventive war being unleashed by American imperialists against the Soviet Union ... (and that) the political aims of the American imperialists are to enslave economically and politically the European and other capitalist countries ... (and) to achieve world domination ... by means of aggressive wars."

Truly, as it was written long ago: "The wicked flee when no man pursueth." Yet it is sad to read these Soviet statements—to realize the extent of the gulf between us. But it is also a warning—a warning to the American people not to fall into the same trap

たらすことでしょう。

　だから，たゆまず努力を続けましょう。平和は必ずしも実現不可能なものではないし，戦争も必ずしも避けられないものではありません。目標をもっとはっきりさせることによって，それをもっと処理しやすい，身近なもののように思わせることによって，われわれは，すべての人々がそれを見，それから希望を得，それに向かって一切の障害を押しのけて力強く進むのを助けることができるのです。

　第二に，ソ連に対するわれわれの態度を再検討しようではありませんか。ソ連宣伝家たちが絶えず書いている通りのことを，ソ連指導者達が実際に信じているかも知れないと思うと，悲観せざるを得ません。軍事戦略に関する最近のソ連の教本を読んで，ページごとに「米帝国主義者は違った形態の戦争を始めようと準備している」とか，「米帝国主義者の政治的目的は，欧州その他の資本主義諸国を経済的，政治的に隷属させ，侵略戦争によって，世界支配を達成するにある」といったような，全く根拠のない途方もない言いがかりが，いろいろ書かれているのを見ると，悲観せざるを得ません。

　まことに昔の書き物にもある通り「邪悪な心を持った者は自分を追跡する者がいない時にでも，逃げまどう」のであります。それにしても，このようなソ連の言い分を読み，米ソ間の間隙がいかに大きいかを知ると，悲観せざるを得ません。しかし，それは同時に警告であり，ソ連と同じような落し穴に陥らないよう，相手方のゆがめられた絶望的な見方だけ見

as the Soviets, not to see only a distorted and desperate view of the other side, not to see conflict as inevitable, accommodation as impossible, and communication as nothing more than an exchange of epithets and threats.

No government or social system is so evil that its people must be considered as lacking in virtue. As Americans, we find Communism profoundly repugnant, as a negation of personal freedom and dignity. But we can still hail the Russian people for their many achievements—in science and space, in economic and industrial growth, in culture, in acts of courage.

Among the many traits the peoples of our two countries have in common, none is stronger than our mutual abhorrence of war. Almost unique among the major world powers, we have never been at war with each other. And no nation in the history of battle ever suffered more than the Russians suffered in the course of the Second World War. At least 20 million lost their lives. Countless millions of homes and farms were burned or sacked. A third of the nation's territory, including nearly two-thirds of its industrial base, was turned into a wasteland—a loss equivalent to the devastation of all this country east of Chicago.

Today, should total war ever break out again—no

ることのないよう，紛争を不可避と考えたり，協調を不可能と見たり，コミュニケーションは形容語や脅し文句の交換以上の何物でもないと思ったりすることがないよう，アメリカ人に警告しているのです。

　政府や社会組織がどんなに悪くても，その国民が道義に欠けていると考えてはなりません。われわれは，米国民として，共産主義は個人の自由と尊厳を否定するので，深くいまわしいものであると思っています。それでもなおわれわれは，科学と宇宙開発，経済と工業の発展，文化や勇敢な行動の面などで，ソ連国民のあげた多くの業績をたたえることができるのです。

　米ソ両国民が共有している幾多の特性のなかで，戦争に対して抱いている嫌悪感ほど強烈なものはありません。大国間では珍しいことですが，米ソ両国は一度も互いに戦争したことはないのです。戦史上，ソ連国民が第二次世界大戦中受けた苦難以上の苦難をなめた国民はかつてありませんでした。この大戦中，ソ連国民の少なくとも二千万人が生命を失いました。数百万戸の住宅や農場が焼かれたり略奪されたりしました。工業地帯の三分の二を含むソ連全領土の三分の一が荒廃に帰しましたが，これはわが国の，シカゴ以東の全域が荒廃に帰したのに相当する損害でありました。

　今日，もし全面戦争が再び起こるようなことがあれば——

matter how—our two countries would be the primary targets. It is an ironic but accurate fact that the two strongest powers are the two in the most danger of devastation. All we have built up, all we have worked for would be destroyed in the first 24 hours. And even in the Cold War—which brings burdens and dangers to so many countries, including this nation's closest allies—our two countries bear the heaviest burdens. For we are both devoting massive sums of money to weapons that could be better devoted to combat ignorance, poverty and disease. We are both caught up in a vicious and dangerous cycle, with suspicion on one side breeding suspicion on the other, and new weapons begetting counter-weapons.

2-14

In short, both the United States and its allies, and the Soviet Union and its allies, have a mutually deep interest in a just and genuine peace and in halting the arms race. Agreements to this end are in the interests of the Soviet Union as well as ours—and even the most hostile nations can be relied upon to accept and keep those treaty obligations, and only those treaty obligations, which are in their own interest.

So let us not be blind to our differences—but let us also direct attention to our common interests and the means by which those differences can be resolved. And if we cannot end now our differences, at least we can help make the world safe for diversity.

たとえそれがどのようにして起きようとも——米ソ両国が互いに主要目標になるのです。最も危険な荒廃の状態にさらされるのは世界最強の両国であるという事実は，皮肉ですが厳然たる事実なのです。われわれがこれまでに努力して築きあげてきたすべてのものが，最初の24時間で破壊されてしまうのであります。そして冷戦においてさえ——冷戦は，米国の最も親密な同盟国を含む多数の国に重荷と危険をもたらしていますが，——最も重い荷を背負っているのは両国であります。なぜならば，両国は共に無知と貧困と病気を克服するために充てることができるはずの巨額の金を，大量の兵器に投じているからです。一方の側の疑惑が他の側の疑惑を生み，新兵器が対抗兵器を生み出すといった危険な悪循環に陥っています。

　要するに，米国とその同盟国およびソ連とその同盟国はともに，真の公正な平和の確立と軍拡競争の停止に，相互に大きな利害を持っているのです。この目的に対する協定は，米国ばかりでなくソ連の利益にもなるのであります。そして，どんなに敵対的な国でも，こうした条約義務，つまり自国の利益になるような条約義務だけは受諾し，順守するでありましょう。

　だから，われわれは両国のもつ相違点に対して，目を向けようではないか，だが，同時に両国共通の利益と，これらの相違点を解消できるような方策に注意を向けようではありませんか。またこれらの相違点を今すぐになくすことはできないにしても，少なくともわれわれは，世界を平穏に存在させる手助けをすることができるでしょう。

> For in the final analysis, our most basic common link is that we all inhabit this small planet. We all breathe the same air. We all cherish our children's futures. And we are all mortal.

Third: let us re-examine our attitude toward the Cold War. Let us remember that we are not engaged in a debate, seeking to pile up debating points. We are not here distributing blame or pointing the finger of judgment. We must deal with the world as it is, and not as it might have been had the history of the last eighteen years been different.

We must, therefore, persevere in the search for peace in the hope that constructive changes within the Communist Bloc might bring within reach solutions which now seem beyond us. We must conduct our affairs in such a way that it becomes in the Communists' interest to agree on a genuine peace. Above all, while always defending our own vital interests, nuclear powers must avert those confrontations which present an adversary with a choice of either a humiliating retreat or a nuclear war. To adopt that kind of course in the nuclear age would be evidence only of the bankruptcy of our policy— or of a collective death-wish for the world.

To secure these ends, America's weapons are non-provocative, carefully controlled, designed to deter, and capable of selective use. Our military forces are

> なぜならば，われわれに共通する最も根本的な絆は，われわれがこの小さな地球に存在しているということです。われわれは皆，同じ空気を吸っているのです。われわれは皆，子孫の将来のことを考えています。そしてわれわれは同じ人間なのです。

　第三に，冷戦に対するわれわれの態度を再検討しようではありませんか。われわれは論争に従事して，得点をかせごうとしているのではないということを自覚しようではありませんか。われわれはまた人々の責任を問うたり，人々を審判したりしているのではありません。われわれはあるがままの世界を対象として考えなければならないのです。もし過去18年間の歴史が違っていたら，こうもなっていたかもしれないと思われるような世界を対象にして考えてはいけないのです。

　それゆえわれわれは，共産圏内部に建設的な変化が起きて，現在は手の届かないように見える解決が手の届くものになることを希望しながら，忍耐強く平和の探求に努めなければならないのです。共産主義者が本当の平和について合意することが，彼らの利益になるようにわれわれは行動しなければなりません。なかんずく，自国の重大な権益を常に擁護しながら，核保有国は，相手国に対して，屈辱的な退却か核戦争かを強いるような対決を避けなければなりません。核時代にこのような方策を採用することは，われわれの政策の破綻を示すものであり，全世界の集団的な死滅を願うことを示すにすぎないのであります。

　以上の目的を完全に果たすために，米国の兵器は挑発的なものではなく，慎重に制御され，抑止用に設計され，選択的に使用できるものになっています。米軍隊は平和を守るため

committed to peace and disciplined in self-restraint. Our diplomats are instructed to avoid unnecessary irritants and purely rhetorical hostility.

For we can seek a relaxation of tensions without relaxing our guard. And, for our part, we do not need to use threats to prove that we are resolute. We do not need to jam foreign broadcasts out of fear our faith will be eroded. We are unwilling to impose our system on any unwilling people—but we are willing and able to engage in peaceful competition with any other system on earth.

Meanwhile, we seek to strengthen the United Nations, to help solve its financial problems, to make it a more effective instrument of peace, to develop it into a genuine world security system—a system capable of resolving disputes on the basis of law, of insuring the security of the large and the small, and of creating conditions under which arms can be finally abolished.

At the same time we seek to keep peace inside the non-Communist world, where many nations, all of them our friends, are divided over issues which weaken Western unity, which invite Communist intervention or which threaten to erupt into war. Our efforts in West New Guinea, in the Congo, in the Middle East and in the Indian subcontinent, have been persistent and patient despite criticism from both sides. We have also tried to set an example for

のものであり，自制することを訓練されています。わが国の外交官は，不必要な刺激と，単なる修辞的な敵対行為を避けるよう教育されています。

　われわれは防衛体制をゆるめないでも緊張の緩和を求めることができるからです。またわれわれとしては，断固とした決意を，実証するために何も脅しを用いる必要はないのです。われわれは，われわれの信念が侵食されることを恐れて，海外からの放送を妨害する必要もありません。われわれは，われわれの制度を，それを欲しない国民に押しつけることは好みません。しかし，われわれは地球上の他のどんな制度とも平和的な競争をすることをはばからないし，また競争することができるのです。

　一方，われわれは国連の強化に，国連の財政上の問題解決に，国連をより効果的な平和の機関にすることに，国連を真の世界安全保障機構，つまり紛争を法に基づいて解決し，大国と小国の双方に安全を保障し，兵器を究極的に廃棄する環境を作り出すことの出来る機構にまで発展させようと努めています。

　同時に，われわれは非共産世界の内側の平和の維持に努めています。非共産世界内部の多くの国が——そのすべてはわれわれの友邦です——いろいろの点で意見の相違を来たして，西側の結束を弱めています。これは共産主義侵略を招き，あるいは戦争を誘発する恐れがあります。西ニューギニア，コンゴ，中東，インド亜大陸におけるわれわれの努力は，双方の側から批判されつつも，根気よく不断につづけられて来ました。われわれはまた，メキシコやカナダなど最も近い隣

others—by seeking to adjust small but significant differences with our own closest neighbors in Mexico and in Canada.

Speaking of other nations, I wish to make one point clear. We are bound to many nations by alliances. Those alliances exist because their concerns and ours substantially overlap. Our commitment to defend Western Europe and West Berlin, for example, stands undiminished because of the identity of our vital interests. The United States will make no deal with the Soviet Union at the expense of other nations and other peoples, not merely because they are our partners, but because their interests and ours converge.

Our interests converge, however, not only in defending the frontiers of freedom, but in pursuing the paths of peace. It is our hope—and the purpose of Allied policies—to convince the Soviet Union that she, too, should let each nation choose its own future, so long as that choice does not interfere with the choices of others. The Communist drive to impose their political and economic system on others is the primary cause of world tension today. For there can be no doubt that, if all nations could refrain from interfering in the self-determination of others, the peace would be much more assured.

This will require a new effort to achieve world law—a new context for world discussions. It will

人との小さいが重大な意見の相違を調整する努力によって，他国に対して一つの模範を示そうと努めてきました。

　他国について述べるにあたり，私はまず，一つの点を明らかにしておきたいのです。われわれは同盟によって多数の国と結ばれています。このような同盟は，これらの国々のもつ利害とわれわれのもつそれとが大幅に重なり合っているために存在しているのであります。たとえば，西欧と西ベルリンを防衛するというわれわれの公約は，軽減されることなく持続しているが，それはわれわれの重大な利害が一致しているためです。米国は，他国や他国民を犠牲にしてソ連と取引きすることはしません。それは，単にそれらの国や国民の利害とわれわれのそれとが一致しているからであります。

　しかし，われわれの利害は単に自由の国々を防衛する点で一致しているだけでなく，平和への道を追求する上でも一致しているのです。われわれの願いは，そして同盟国の政策の目的は，各国に自国の将来を選択するにあたり他国の選択を侵害しない限り，各国に自国の将来を選択させるべきであることをソ連に納得させようとすることであります。自分達の政治経済体制を他国に押しつけようとする共産主義者の運動は，今日の世界緊張の主な原因です。なぜなら，すべての国が他国の自決の妨害を差しひかえるなら，平和がはるかによく保障されることは疑う余地がないからであります。

　そのためには世界法，すなわち世界的な討議のための新しい環境を造り上げる新たな努力が必要となりましょう。それ

require increased understanding between the Soviets and ourselves. And increased understanding will require increased contact and communication. One step in this direction is the proposed arrangement for a direct line between Moscow and Washington, to avoid on each side the dangerous delays, misunderstandings, and misreadings of the other's actions which might occur in a time of crisis.

We have also been talking in Geneva about other first-step measures of arms control, designed to limit the intensity of the arms race and to reduce the risks of accidental war. Our primary long-range interest in Geneva, however, is general and complete disarmament—designed to take place by stages, permitting parallel political developments to build the new institutions of peace which would take the place of arms. The pursuit of disarmament has been an effort of this government since the 1920's. It has been urgently sought by the past three administrations. And however dim the prospects are today, we intend to continue this effort—to continue it in order that all countries, including our own, can better grasp what the problems and the possibilities of disarmament are.

The only major area of these negotiations where the end is in sight—yet where a fresh start is badly needed—is in a treaty to outlaw nuclear tests. The conclusion of such a treaty—so near and yet so far

にはソ連とわれわれ自身との間のもっと深い理解が必要となるでありましょう。そしてこの理解を深めるためには，接触と意思の疎通を増進することが必要となります。この方向へ向かっての第一歩は，危機のさいにおこりかねない，相手方の行動に対する危険な遅滞，誤解，誤読を避けるために提案された，モスクワ・ワシントン間の直通通信線の設置であります。

　われわれはこの他にもジュネーブで，激化する軍備競争を制限し，偶発戦争の危険を減ずることを目的とする他の軍備管理への第一段階措置について話し合ってきました。しかし，ジュネーブにおけるわれわれの第一の遠大な関心事は全面完全軍縮です。それは，これと平行する政治的進展によって軍備に代わる新しい平和機構が打ち立てられるべく段階を追って実施するよう立案されたものです。軍縮は1920年代以来，わが国の政府が努力して追求してきたものです。これまで三代にわたり，政府は熱心にこれを求めてきました。そして，今日，見通しがたとえどんなにかすかであろうとも，われわれは努力を続けるつもりであります。われわれ自身を含めてすべての国々が，軍縮の問題と可能性とはどんなものであるかをよりよく理解できるよう，努力を続けていくつもりです。

　これらの交渉で，目標は目の前に見えていながら，しかも新たな出発が切実に必要とされている唯一の主要な分野は，核実験を禁止する条約です。このような条約の締結は，目の前にあって，しかも極めて遠いのですが，軍備競争のうちで

—would check the spiraling arms race in one of its most dangerous areas. It would place the nuclear powers in a position to deal more effectively with one of the greatest hazards which man faces in 1963—the further spread of nuclear arms. It would increase our security—it would decrease the prospects of war. Surely this goal is sufficiently important to require our steady pursuit, yielding neither to the temptation to give up the whole effort nor the temptation to give up our insistence on vital and responsible safeguards.

I am taking this opportunity, therefore, to announce two important decisions in this regard:

First: Chairman Khrushchev, Prime Minister Macmillan and I have agreed that high-level discussions will shortly begin in Moscow looking towards early agreement on a comprehensive test ban treaty. Our hopes must be tempered with the caution of history—but with our hopes go the hopes of all mankind.

Second: to make clear our good faith and solemn convictions on this matter, I now declare that the United States does not propose to conduct nuclear tests in the atmosphere so long as other states do not do so. We will not be the first to resume. Such a declaration is no substitute for a formal, binding treaty—but I hope it will help us achieve one. Nor would such a treaty be a substitute for disarmament—but I hope it will help us achieve it.

最も危険な領域における軍備競争の激化を阻止することになります。このような条約によって核保有国は，1963年に人間が直面する最大の危険の一つ，核兵器のこれ以上の拡散をより効果的に処理することができる立場に置かれています。それはわれわれの安全を増し，戦争の恐れを少なくするにちがいありません。この目標は，あらゆる努力を放棄しようとする誘惑にも，また，死ぬか生きるかを決めるほどに重要な安全保障措置についての主張を放棄しようとする誘惑にも屈しない，着実な努力を必要とするほど重要なものであることは言うまでもありません。

そこで，この機会を利用してこれに関連した二つの重要な決定を発表します。

第一に，フルシチョフ・ソ連首相とマクミラン英首相と私は，包括的な核実験停止条約を早期に締結するために，近くモスクワで高級会談を開くことで意見の一致をみました。われわれは歴史の警告に従って，これに過大の期待を寄せることをさし控えなければなりませんが，われわれの期待は，また全人類の期待でもあります。

第二に，この件に関するわれわれの誠意と厳粛な信念を明らかにするために，私は他国がしない限り，米国は大気圏での核実験をしないことを宣言します。われわれは実験を再開する最初の国にはなりません。こうした宣言は，拘束力ある正式の条約に代わるものではありませんが，これが条約の達成の助けになることを期待しています。またこうした条約は軍縮の代わりにならないかも知れませんが，その実現の助けになることでしょう。

Finally, my fellow Americans, let us re-examine our attitude toward peace and freedom here at home. The quality and spirit of our own society must justify and support our efforts abroad. We must show it in the dedication of our own lives—as many of you who are graduating today will have a unique opportunity to do, by serving without pay in the Peace Corps abroad or in the proposed National Service Corps here at home.

But wherever we are, we must all, in our daily lives, live up to the age-old faith that peace and freedom walk together. In too many of our cities today, the peace is not secure because freedom is incomplete.

It is the responsibility of the Executive Branch at all levels of government—local, state and national—to provide and protect that freedom for all citizens by all means within their authority. It is the responsibility of the Legislative Branch at all levels wherever that authority is not now adequate, to make it adequate. And it is the responsibility of all citizens in all sections to respect the rights of all others and to respect the law of the land.

All this is not unrelated to world peace. "When a man's ways please the Lord," the Scriptures tell us, "he maketh even his enemies to be at peace with him." And is not peace, in the last analysis, basically

国民諸君，最後に，国内の平和と自由に対するわれわれの態度を再検討してみましょう。われわれ自身の社会の質と精神は，海外でのわれわれの努力を正当化し，支えるようなものでなければなりません。われわれは自らの生活をささげることによってこれを示さなければなりません。本日卒業される諸君の多くは，海外派遣の平和部隊や，現在提案されている国民奉仕隊に無給で奉仕することによって，これを行なうまたとない機会をもたれることと思います。

　しかし，たとえどこに居りましょうとも，われわれは皆，平和と自由は相伴うものであるという，古くからの信念に従って生きてゆかねばなりません。今日わが国におきましては，あまりにも多くの都市で，自由が不完全なために平和が確立しておりません。

　権限の許容範囲内のあらゆる手段を用いることによって，すべての市民に自由を与え，これを擁護することは，地方，州，国家を問わず，あらゆるレベルでの行政府の責任であり，またこの権限が現在十分でない場合，これを十分なものにすることは，あらゆるレベルでの立法府の責任であります。そして，他のすべての人の権利と国法を尊重することは，あらゆる地域のあらゆる市民の責任です。

　以上のことは世界平和に無関係なものではありません。聖書に「人の道が主を喜ばせる時，主はその人の敵をもその人と和らがせられる」と述べています。平和は結局のところ，根本的には人権，すなわち踏みにじられる恐れなしに生活を

a matter of human rights—the right to live out our lives without fear of devastation—the right to breathe air as nature provided it—the right of future generations to a healthy existence?

While we proceed to safeguard our national interests, let us also safeguard human interests. And the elimination of war and arms is clearly in the interest of both. No treaty, however much it may be to the advantage of all, however tightly it may be worded, can provide absolute security against the risks of deception and evasion. But it can—if it is sufficiently effective in its enforcement and if it is sufficiently in the interests of its signers—offer far more security and far fewer risks than an unabated, uncontrolled, unpredictable arms race.

The United States, as the world knows, will never start a war. We do not want a war. We do not now expect a war. This generation of Americans has already had enough—more than enough—of war and hate and oppression. We shall be prepared for war, if others wish it. We shall be alert to try to stop it. But we shall also do our part to build a world of peace where the weak are safe and the strong are just. We are not helpless before that task or hopeless of its success. Confident and unafraid, we labor on—not toward a strategy of annihilation but toward a strategy of peace.

全うする権利，自然が与えたままの空気を呼吸する権利，将来の世代が健全な生存を続けうる権利の問題ではないでしょうか。

　われわれは，わが国家利益を擁護していく一方，人間の利益も擁護しようではありませんか。戦争と軍備の廃棄は，明らかにこの二つを利するものです。条約というものは，どれほど大きな利益を万人に与えるものであっても，どれほど厳格な条文で規定されているものであっても，偽瞞や回避の危険に対する絶対的な保証とはなりえません。しかし，条約は，もしそれが実施上十分効果的であり，十分締結国の利益になる場合は，不断の無統制な予断しがたい軍備競争より，はるかに大きな安全を与え，危険がはるかに緩和されるのです。

　世界が知っているように，米国は決して戦争を始めることをしません。われわれは戦争を欲していないのです。現在戦争を予期してもいません。現代の米国民は，戦争や憎悪や圧迫にはすでに飽き飽きしているのです。もし他国が戦争を欲するなら，われわれも戦争に備えるでありましょう。戦争が起こらないよう十分警戒するでありましょう。しかし，われわれは弱国が安全であり，強国が公正である平和な世界を築き上げるために，われわれの分を尽くすつもりであります。われわれはそのような任務を前にして無力ではなく，その成功に絶望しているのでもないのです。自信を持ち，恐れることなく，われわれは人類壊滅の戦略に向かってではなく，平和の戦略に向かって努力し続けるのです。

BANNING NUCLEAR TESTS

Good evening, my fellow citizens:

I speak to you tonight in a spirit of hope. Eighteen years ago the advent of nuclear weapons changed the course of the world, as well as the war. Since that time, all mankind has been struggling to escape from the darkening prospects of mass destruction on earth. In an age when both sides have come to possess enough nuclear power to destroy the human race several times over, the world of Communism and the world of free choice have been caught up in a vicious circle of conflicting ideology and interests. Each increase of tension has produced an increase of arms; each increase of arms has produced an increase of tension.

In these years, the United States and the Soviet Union have frequently communicated suspicions and warnings to each other, but very rarely hope. Our representatives have met at the summit, and at the brink; they have met in Washington and in Moscow, in Geneva, and at the United Nations. But too often these meetings have produced only darkness, discord, or disillusion.

核実験停止条約に関する演説

　皆さん今晩は。
　今日は皆さんに希望の気持をこめてお話しします。18年前に核兵器が作られ，そのために戦争のあり方はもちろん，世界のあり方も変わってしまいました。その時以来全人類は，いつの日か大崩壊が起こるのではないかという暗い予感が現実にならないように，一生懸命努力し続けてきました。双方が全人類を数回以上も絶滅させて余りある核兵器を保有するに到った今，共産主義国と自由主義国は，イデオロギーと利益が衝突するという悪循環に巻きこまれてきました。緊張が増すごとに軍備も拡張されてきましたし，軍備が拡張されるとまた緊張が増す，といった状態にありました。
　ここ数年間，合衆国とソビエトは，お互いに疑念や警告を何度となく伝え合ってきたのですが，残念ながら望み薄でした。両国の代表は，緊張緩和状態の時も，緊張状態の時も会ってきました。ワシントンで，モスクワで，ジュネーブで，そして国連で会って来ました。しかしこれらの会議は暗い見通しに終わり，何も合意に達せず，幻滅を感じさせるだけでした。

Yesterday, a shaft of light cut into the darkness. Negotiations were concluded in Moscow on a treaty to ban all nuclear tests in the atmosphere, in outer space, and underwater. For the first time, an agreement has been reached on bringing the forces of nuclear destruction under international control—a goal first sought in 1946 when Bernard Baruch presented a comprehensive control plan to the United Nations.

   That plan, and many subsequent disarmament plans, large and small, have all been blocked by those opposed to international inspection. A ban on nuclear tests, however, requires on-the-spot inspection only for underground tests. This nation now possesses a variety of techniques to detect the nuclear tests of other nations which are conducted in the air or underwater. For such tests produce unmistakable signs which our modern instruments can pick up.

   The treaty initialed yesterday, therefore, is a limited treaty which permits continued underground testing and prohibits only those tests that we ourselves can police. It requires no control posts, no on-site inspections, no international body.

   We should also understand that it has other limits as well. Any nation which signs the treaty will have an opportunity to withdraw if it finds that extraordinary events related to the subject matter of the treaty

ところが昨日，一条の陽光が暗やみに差し込んできました。モスクワでの交渉の結果，大気圏内，大気圏外，及び水中での核実験を禁止する条約が妥結されたのです。初めて核兵器戦力を世界レベルで抑制する協定が妥結しました。それは，1946年に米国のバーナード・バルーク代表が国連に包括的な抑制計画を提出した時に，最初に提案された目標であります。

　バルーク代表の計画や，それ以後に提出された軍備縮少計画は，その規模に関係なく，国際査察に反対する国々によって，すべて反対され続けてきました。しかしこの核実験禁止については，現地査察を必要とするのは地下実験についてのみです。わが国は今や種々の技術を開発しており，他国が大気圏内や水中で核実験を行っても探知することができます。これらの実験では明らかな形跡が残るため，われわれの近代的装備が見つけ出せるのです。

　それゆえ，昨日妥結された条約は，われわれが取り締まることができる実験のみを禁止するものであり，今後も地下実験を続けることは可能です。また監視所や正規の査察団，国際的組織をもこの条約は規定していません。

　これ以外にも許可されていることがあるということを知っておく必要があります。この条約に署名をしたどの国も，この条約の主目標に関して，何か重大な出来事が起こり，国家

have jeopardized its supreme interests; and no nation's right of self-defense will in any way be impaired. Nor does this treaty mean an end to the threat of nuclear war. It will not reduce nuclear stockpiles; it will not halt the production of nuclear weapons; it will not restrict their use in time of war.

Nevertheless, this limited treaty will radically reduce the nuclear testing which would otherwise be conducted on both sides; it will prohibit the United States, the United Kingdom, the Soviet Union and all others who sign it from engaging in atmospheric tests which have so alarmed mankind; and it offers to all the world a welcome sign of hope.

For this is not a unilateral moratorium, but a specific and solemn legal obligation. While it will not prevent this nation from testing underground, or from being ready to resume atmospheric tests if the acts of others so require, it gives us a concrete opportunity to extend its coverage to other nations and later to other forms of nuclear tests.

This treaty is in part the product of Western patience and vigilance. We have made clear—most recently in Berlin and in Cuba—our deep resolve to protect our security and our freedom against any threat or aggression. We have also made clear our steadfast determination to limit the arms race. In three administrations, our soldiers and diplomats have

の究極の利益が危くなったら，いつでも脱退できるし，自国を守る権利はいかなる方法でも奪われるものではありません。また，この条約が妥結したために核戦争の脅威がなくなったということではありませんし，核の貯蔵量が減るわけでもありません。核兵器の製造が中止されるわけでもなければ，戦争が起こった場合に核兵器の使用を禁止するものでもありません。

　しかしながら，この部分的条約のおかげで，今後双方で行なわれるであろう核実験は，大幅に減ると思われます。また，この条約に署名した，アメリカ，イギリス，ソビエト及び他の国々は，今まで人類に脅威を与えてきた大気圏内の核実験を禁止するでしょう。このように世界中に希望が持てるという明るいきざしを投げかけています。

　というのも，この条約は，全面的な核実験停止ではありませんが，はっきりと限定された厳然たる法律的協定であるからです。この条約は，他国の行為の結果，もし必要ならば，わが国が地下実験をすることを禁止したり，大気圏内の実験を再開する準備をするのを禁止しているわけではありません。将来，その適応範囲を他の国々の核実験に対し，また他の核実験方法に対して及ぼすための具体的な機会を与えております。

　この条約はある意味では，西欧諸国の忍耐と警戒の結果，妥結されたものです。われわれは新しくはベルリン，キューバにおいて，どんな脅威や攻撃からもわれわれの安全と自由を守る，という心からの決意を明らかにしてきました。さらに軍備拡張競争を制限しようという，確固たる決意も表明してきました。3つの国の政府内で，われわれの軍人と外交官

worked together to this end, always with the support of Great Britain. Prime Minister Macmillan joined with President Eisenhower in proposing a limited test ban treaty in 1959, and again with me in 1961 and 1962.

But the achievement of this goal is not a victory for one side—it is a victory for mankind. It reflects no concessions either to or by the Soviet Union. It reflects simply our common recognition of the dangers in further testing.

This treaty is not the millennium. It will not resolve all conflicts, or cause the Communists to forego their ambitions, or eliminate the dangers of war. It will not reduce our need for arms or allies or programs of assistance to others. But it is an important first step—a step toward peace—a step toward reason —a step away from war.

Here is what this step can mean to you and your children and your neighbors.

First, this treaty can be a step toward reduced world tensions and broader areas of agreement. The Moscow talks reached agreement on no other subject, nor is this treaty conditioned on any other matter. Under-Secretary Harriman made it clear that any non-aggression arrangements across the division in Europe would require full consultation with our allies and full attention to their interests. He

が，英国の支持を受けて，この目的のために働いてきました。1959年に，マクミラン首相がアイゼンハワー大統領と共に核実験禁止条約を提唱し，後には私も加わって，1961年と1962年に再度提唱しました。この目的を達成したからと言って，それは，一方が他方に勝ったのだ，とかいうレベルの問題ではないのです。それは人類にとっての勝利なのです。またアメリカがソビエトに譲歩したというのでもなければ，その逆でもないのです。これ以上核実験をすることは危険であるという両側の，共通の認識を反映しただけなのです。

　この条約が成立したとは言え，絶対的平和の到来を告げるものではありません。この条約によってすべての衝突が解決できるのでもなく，また共産主義者が野心を捨てるのでもなければ，戦争の危険性がなくなるわけでもありません。しかしこの条約は，戦争回避への，人間の良識への，そして平和への意味ある最初の一歩と言えるものです。

　さて，ここでこの条約が，皆さん，及び皆さんの子孫にとって，どういう意味を持っているのかお話ししましょう。

　まず第一に，この条約は，世界の緊張を緩和し，合意に達する範囲をもっと広げる第一歩になり得るということです。モスクワ会談では，他のどんな主題も，合意に達することができませんでした。この条約は他のどんな事態にも左右されることはないのです。ハリソン長官のもとで，ヨーロッパ中の国境を超えて，侵略をされない協定を作るためには，同盟国間で充分な協議をし，各国の利益に対し，充分な注意を払わなくてはならないだろうということが明らかにされました。

also made clear our strong preference for a more comprehensive treaty banning all tests everywhere, and our ultimate hope for general and complete disarmament. The Soviet Government, however, is still unwilling to accept the inspection such goals require.

No one can predict with certainty, therefore, what further agreements, if any, can be built on the foundations of this one. They could include controls on preparations for surprise attack, or on numbers and types of armaments. There could be further limitations on the spread of nuclear weapons. The important point is that efforts to seek new agreement will go forward.

But the difficulty of predicting the next step is no reason to be reluctant about this one. Nuclear test ban negotiations have long been a symbol of East-West disagreement. If this treaty can also be a symbol—if it can symbolize the end of one era and the beginning of another—if both sides can by this treaty gain confidence and experience in peaceful collaboration—then this short and simple treaty may well become an historic mark in man's age-old pursuit of peace.

Western policies have long been designed to persuade the Soviet Union to renounce aggression, direct or indirect, so that their people and all people may

また彼は，核実験を禁止するもっと包括的な条約を強く望むわれわれの意向と，全面的かつ完全に武装解除しようとするわれわれの究極的な目標を明らかにしました。ところがソビエト政府は，このような目的達成に必要な査察をまだ受け入れようとはしていません。

　これが現状ですから，今後，もしあるとしたら，どんな条約がこの条約をもとにして作られるのか，全く予想できません。それらは奇襲の準備を抑制したり，軍備の規模や種類を抑制するものである可能性はあります。また核兵器拡散をもっと強く禁止するものであるかも知れません。が，大事なことは，新しく協定を結ぼうとする努力を続けて行くことなのです。

　しかし，次にどういう進展が見られるのか予測するのが難しいのです。なぜなら，今回の条約に同意するのに不承不承である理由がないはずなのに，実際ここまで難航したからです。核実験停止交渉が行なわれ続けてきたことは，長い間，西側と東側の間で意見の相違があったことを示す象徴でした。もしこの条約を結んだことが，一つの象徴になり得るのなら，もし一つの時代の終りと次なる時代の始まりを象徴するのなら，もし両側がこの条約を結んだことによって平和実現のために協力し合ったのであるという自信と経験になり得るのなら，この短い簡単な条約も人類が平和を追い求める長い歴史の中の一歩となるでありましょう。

　長い間，西側の政策は，お互いの国民が平和に生きてゆくために，直接的にしろ間接的にしろ，攻撃をひかえるよう，

live and let live in peace. The unlimited testing of new weapons of war cannot lead toward that end—but this treaty, if it can be followed by further progress, can clearly move in that direction.

5 I do not say that a world without aggression or threats of war would be an easy world. It will bring new problems, new challenges from the Communists, new dangers of relaxing our vigilance or of mistaking their intent.

10 But those dangers pale in comparison to those of the spiralling arms race and a collision course toward war. Since the beginning of history, war has been mankind's constant companion. It has been the rule, not the exception. Even a nation as young and peace-
15 loving as our own has fought through eight wars. And three times in the last two and a half years I have been required to report to you as President that this nation and the Soviet Union stood on the verge of direct military confrontation—in Laos, in Berlin and
20 in Cuba.

A war today or tomorrow, if it led to nuclear war, would not be like any war in history. A full-scale nuclear exchange, lasting less than 60 minutes, with the weapons now in existence, could wipe out more than 300
25 million Americans, Europeans and Russians, as well as untold millions elsewhere. And the survivors, as Chairman Khrushchev warned the Communist Chinese,

ソビエトに説得する内容のものでありました。もし戦争に使う新兵器を無制限に実験し続けたら，この目的を達成することは不可能ですが，この条約によって，今後いっそうの進展が見られたら，この目的に一歩でも近づくことは明らかです。

　私は，攻撃や戦争の脅威がなくなれば，この世界は暮らしやすくなるであろうとは思いません。なぜならば，今までになかった新しい問題が生じるでしょうし，共産主義者は別の方法で攻撃をしかけてくるかもしれず，またわれわれが警戒の手をゆるめてしまうために新たな危険が生じるでしょうし，共産主義者のねらいを誤って解釈する危険性も生じると思われるからです。

　しかしこれらがもたらす危険は，悪循環となっている軍備拡張競争や戦争への道をたどることの危険性に比べると，まだ少ないものです。有史以来，戦争はいつも人間とその軌跡を共にしてきました。戦争はいつも世の常であって，特例的なことではなかったのです。われわれの国のようにまだ歴史も浅く，平和を愛する国であっても，今までに 8 回もの戦争を経験してきました。この 2 年半の間にも 3 回，私は大統領として，わが国とソビエトはラオスで，ベルリンで，キューバで今にも直接的に軍事衝突をしそうなところでした，と皆さんに報告する必要があったのです。

　もし今日，および未来に戦争が起こり，それが核戦争にまで発展したら，歴史上例を見ないようなすさまじいものとなるでありましょう。全面核戦争になったら，今ある核兵器で一時間以内に各地で数えきれないほどの死者が出るのはもちろんのこと，3 億人を超えるアメリカ人，ヨーロッパ人，ロシア人が死んでしまうでしょう。そして生存者も，フルシチョフ首相が中国に対して警告したように「生存者は死んだ

"the survivors would envy the dead," for they would inherit a world so devastated by explosions and poison and fire that today we cannot even conceive of its horrors.

So let us try to turn the world away from war. Let us make the most of this opportunity, and every opportunity, to reduce tension, to slow down the perilous nuclear arms race, and to check the world's slide toward final annihilation.

Second, this treaty can be a step toward freeing the world from the fears and dangers of radioactive fallout. Our own atmospheric tests last year were conducted under conditions which restricted such fallout to an absolute minimum. But over the years, the number and the yield of weapons tested have rapidly increased—and so have the radioactive hazards from such testing, continued, unrestricted testing, by the nuclear powers, joined in time by other nations, which may be less adept in limiting pollution, will increasingly contaminate the air that all of us must breathe.

Even then, the number of children and grandchildren with cancer in their bones, with leukemia in their blood, or with poison in their lungs might seem statistically small to some, in comparison with natural health hazards. But this is not a natural health hazard—and it is not a statistical issue. The loss of

者をうらやましがる」でしょう。というのも，そうなった時には，この世界は核爆発や放射能，それに閃光等で，今日われわれがそれがどんなに恐しいものか想像もできないくらいに荒廃してしまうでしょうから。

　だからこそ，この世界から戦争をなくすよう努力しましょう。この機会を，またすべての機会を最大限にとらえて，緊張を緩和し，危険な核兵器拡張競争をおさえ，全世界が人類絶滅という終局に向かわないように注意しようではありませんか。

　二番目に，この条約は全世界の人口を放射性物質が降下するという恐怖や危険性から救う一歩となり得るでしょう。われわれが昨年度に行った実験では，放射性物質の降下を最少限度に抑えるという条件つきでした。が，実験された核兵器の数や爆発力は，この数年間で急速に増加し，その結果，核大国による継続的無制限の実験だけでも，放射能汚染の危険性はますます増加しています。これにもし汚染を抑えることにあまり熟練していない国々がしだいに実験を始めだすとすると，われわれが生きて行くために呼吸しなくてはならない空気は，もっと汚染されることになるでしょう。

　そうなったとしても，骨にガンができたり，白血病になったり，肺に腫ようができたりする子孫達の数は，自然にそうなる場合の数に比べて，統計的にはあまり増えないように思えるかもしれません。しかし，これは放射能汚染によるもので，自然に健康を害したのではありませんし，数字の上での問題でもありません。核兵器のために一人でも人間の命が失われることがあったり，われわれが死んでしまったずっと後で生まれた子供に，一人でも奇形児がいたりしたら，われわ

even one human life, or the malformation of even one baby—who may be born long after all of us have gone—should be of concern to us all. Our children and grandchildren are not merely statistics toward which we can be indifferent.

Nor does this affect the nuclear powers alone. These tests befoul the air of all men and all nations, the committed and the uncommitted alike, without their knowledge, and without their consent. That is why the continuation of atmospheric testing causes so many countries to regard all nuclear powers as equally evil; and we can hope that its prevention will enable those countries to see the world more clearly, while enabling all the world to breathe more easily.

Third, this treaty can be a step towards preventing the spread of nuclear weapons to nations not now possessing them. During the next several years, in addition to the four current nuclear powers, a small but significant number of nations will have the intellectual, physical and financial resources to produce both nuclear weapons and the means of delivering them. In time, it is estimated, many other nations will have either this capacity or other ways of obtaining nuclear warheads, even as missiles can be commercially purchased today.

I ask you to stop and think for a moment what it would mean to have nuclear weapons in so many

れすべてに責任があるのです。われわれの子孫のことは，単なる統計上の問題として無関心でいてもいい，というものではありません。

このようなことは核保有国にのみ起こるのではありません。これらの実験を行なえば，全人類の，全国家——実験をした国はもちろん，していない国も含めて——のものである空気が，誰にも知らされず，誰の同意も得ずに汚染されることになるのです。だからこそ，大気圏内で実験を続けることを，多くの国が，実験自体はもちろんのこと，核を保有する国も悪であると考えているのです。それでもし実験が禁止されたら，世界の人々がもっと楽に呼吸できるのはもちろんのこと，こういった国々も世界をもっと楽観的に見るようになるでありましょう。

第3に，この条約は，核兵器が今それを保有していない国にまで拡散されるのを防ぐことに向けての一歩となり得ることです。数年後には，現在の核保有国4ヵ国に加えて，そんなに多くではないとしても，かなりの数の国が核兵器を作り，それを発射する設備を整え得る頭脳と物質，それに経済力を所持することになるでありましょう。近いうちに多くの国家がこういった能力を持つか，それ以外の方法で核弾頭を得るでありましょう。今日ではミサイルもお金を出せば買えるのですから。

皆さん，ちょっとここで考えてみて下さい。もし多くの国が核を保有したら，いったいどうなるのか。大国も小国も，安定している国も不安定な国も，責任ある国もない国も含め

hands—in the hands of countries large and small, stable and unstable, responsible and irresponsible, scattered throughout the world. There would be no rest for anyone then, no stability, no real security, and no chance of effective disarmament. There would only be the increased chance of accidental war, and an increased necessity for the great powers to involve themselves in what otherwise would be local conflicts.

If only one thermonuclear bomb were to be dropped on any American, Russian or any other city—whether it was launched by accident or design, by a madman or by an enemy, by a large nation or by a small, from any corner of the world—that one bomb could release more destructive power on the inhabitants of that one helpless city than all the bombs dropped in the Second World War.

Neither the United States, nor the Soviet Union, nor the United Kingdom, nor France can look forward to that day with equanimity. We have a great obligation—all four nuclear powers have a great obligation to use whatever time remains to prevent the spread of nuclear weapons, to persuade other countries not to test, transfer, acquire, possess or produce such weapons.

This treaty can be the opening wedge in that campaign. It provides that none of the parties will assist

> て世界中に……。もしそうなれば，誰も気を安めることはできないでありましょうし，政治的安定状態も，本当の防衛も，効果的な軍備縮少の機会もないでしょう。そこにあるものは偶発戦争が起こる可能性が増加することと，大国が局地的衝突に加わる必要性が増加することくらいのものです。
>
> 　もし，たった一つでも水素爆弾がアメリカ，ロシア，もしくは他の都市に落とされることがあれば，たとえそれが偶然の発射であれ，意図的な発射であれ，狂人のしわざであれ，敵によるものであれ，また世界のどこの大国からであれ，小国からであれ，その一発で，不幸にもその都市は第二次世界大戦中に落とされたすべての爆弾以上の力で破壊されるでありましょう。

　合衆国も，ソビエトも，イギリスもフランスも，何もしないでその日が来るのを待っているはずがありません。われわれは重要な協定を結びました。それは4つの核保有国は，残されたいかなる時間も，核兵器の拡散を禁止し，他の国にもそのような実験をしたり，運びこんだり，手に入れたり，所有したり，造ったりしないように説得するために使うというものです。

　この条約はその運動への第一歩となり得ます。というのもどの政党も，他国が禁止している環境で実験することを援助しない，と規定しているからです。またこの条約は，今後核兵器抑制に関する協定をもっと結ぶための門戸を開放しました。どの国家もいつでも署名できるのです。これはすべての

other nations to test in the forbidden environments. It opens the door for further agreements on the control of nuclear weapons. And it is open for all nations to sign. For it is in the interest of all nations—and already we have heard from a number of countries who wish to join with us promptly.

Fourth, and finally, this treaty can limit the nuclear arms race in many ways, which, on balance, will strengthen our nation's security far more than the continuation of unrestricted testing. For in today's world, a nation's security does not always increase as its arms increase, when its adversary is doing the same. And unlimited competition in the testing and development of new types of destructive nuclear weapons will not make the world safer for either side.

Under this limited treaty, on the other hand, the testing of other nations could never be sufficient to offset the ability of our strategic forces to deter or survive a nuclear attack and to penetrate and destroy an aggressor's homeland. We have, and under this treaty we will continue to have, all the nuclear strength that we need.

It is true that the Soviets have tested nuclear weapons of a yield higher than that which we have thought to be necessary; but the hundred megaton bomb of which they spoke two years ago does not and will not change the balance of strategic power.

国家にとっても利益になるのです。事実すでに多くの国からすぐに加わりたいという声を聞いています。

　最後になりますが第4番目として，この条約は，結局無制限に実験を続けるよりも，もっとわが国の国防力を高めてくれるいろいろな方法で核兵器拡張競争を制限する可能性があります。というのも，今日のような世界では，ある国が軍備拡張をしても敵対国が同じことをすれば，必ずしも防衛力を拡張したことにならないからです。そして，新しい破壊力を備えた核兵器の実験と開発の競争が無制限に行なわれると，世界はどちら側にとってもより安全ではなくなるでしょう。

　一方，この制限条約のもとで他国が実験をしたとしても，われわれの戦略，軍の核攻撃を防いだり，切り抜けたり，敵国を攻撃，破壊する能力に追いつくことはないでしょう。われわれは，この条約下で必要最少限の核を保有し続けます。

　確かにソビエトは必要と思われる以上の爆発力を持った核実験を行ないました。しかし彼らが2年前に話していた100メガトン規模の爆弾をもってしても，戦略軍の力関係は変わっていませんし，これからも変わらないでしょう。合衆国は慎重に考え，以前よりは低いが充分な爆発力があり，もっと機動力に富む，より効果的な兵器を作ることに精力を注ぐこ

The United States has deliberately chosen to concentrate on more mobile and more efficient weapons, with lower but entirely sufficient yield; and our security is not, therefore, impaired by the treaty I am discussing.

It is also true, as Mr. Khrushchev would agree, that nations cannot afford in these matters to rely simply on the good faith of their adversaries. We have not, therefore, overlooked the risk of secret violations. There is at present a possibility that deep in outer space, that hundreds and thousands and millions of miles away from the earth, illegal tests might go undetected. But we already have the capability to construct a system of observation that would make such tests almost impossible to conceal, and we can decide at any time whether such a system is needed in the light of the limited risk to us and the limited reward to others of violations attempted at that range. For any tests which might be conducted so far out in space, which cannot be conducted more easily and efficiently and legally underground, would necessarily be of such a magnitude that they would be extremely difficult to conceal. We can also employ new devices to check on the testing of smaller weapons in the lower atmosphere. Any violation, moreover, involves, along with the risk of detection, the end of the treaty and world-wide consequences for

とを選んできました。従ってわれわれの防衛力は今お話ししているような脅威によっても変わることはありません。

　また，フルシチョフ首相も同じ考えだと思いますが，どの国家も軍事問題については敵国が忠実に義務を守ってくれると一方的に信ずるわけにはいかないのです。だからわれわれは，秘密裏に違法行為がなされているという危険があることを見落としていません。現在でも，地球から離れること，はるか数百，数千億マイル先の外宇宙で，不法実験が探知されずに行なわれている可能性がないわけではありません。しかし，われわれはすでに監視装置を完成させる能力があり，完成してしまえば，秘密裏に実験を行なうことはほとんど不可能になるでしょう。他国がそのように離れた距離で不法実験を行なった場合，われわれに与える危険性があまりなく，実験を行なった国にとってもあまり得るものがないということを考えてみて，そのような装置が必要かどうか，いつでも決めることができます。というのも，そんな宇宙の外れで実験が行なわれたとしたら，それは地下でも簡単に，効果的かつ合法的には行なえない実験で，隠すのが極度に困難なくらいの規模のものであるはずです。対流圏内で小規模実験が行なわれたかどうかを調査する装置も作ろうと思えば作れます。どんな違反実験が行なわれた場合も探知される危険性があるのはもちろん，それは条約破棄を意味し，違反国に対する世界的な非難も当然あるでしょう。

the violator.

Secret violations are possible and secret preparations for a sudden withdrawal are possible, and, thus, our own vigilance and strength must be maintained, as we remain ready to withdraw and to resume all forms of testing, if we must. But it would be a mistake to assume that this treaty will be quickly broken. The gains of illegal testing are obviously slight compared to their cost and the hazard of discovery, and the nations which have initialed and will sign this treaty prefer it, in my judgment, to unrestricted testing as a matter of their own self-interest, for these nations, too, and all nations, have a stake in limiting the arms race, in holding the spread of nuclear weapons, and in breathing air that is not radioactive. While it may be theoretically possible to demonstrate the risks inherent in any treaty, and such risks in this treaty are small, the far greater risks to our security are the risks of unrestricted testing, the risk of a nuclear arms race, the risk of new nuclear powers, nuclear pollution, and nuclear war.

This limited test ban, in our most careful judgment, is safer by far for the United States than an unlimited nuclear arms race. For all these reasons, I am hopeful that this nation will promptly approve the limited test ban treaty. There will, of course, be debate in the country and in the Senate. The Constitution

秘密裏に違反行為をしたり，隠れて脱退の準備をすることは可能です。だからわれわれは，必要とあればいつでも脱退し，種々の実験を再開できるようにして警戒，強化を続けなくてはいけません。しかし，この条約がすぐに破棄されるものだとお考えでしたら，それは間違いでしょう。不法に実験を行なっても得るであろうものは，かかった費用や発見される危険性を考えてみると明らかに少ないし，この条約に署名をした国やこれから署名をするであろう国は，利己主義の産物である無制限な核実験よりも条約の方を選んでいるのです。というのもこれらの国はもちろん，すべての国は軍備拡大競争を制限したり，核兵器が世界中に広まるのを抑えたり，放射能を含まない空気を吸ったりすることにより利益を受けるからです。確かに理論的にはどの条約にも初めから危険性が含まれていますが，この条約について言えばそのような危険性は小さいのに対し，無制限に実験が行なわれることや，核兵器拡大競争や，新しく核保有国が生まれ，新しい核汚染が始まり，核戦争が起こる可能性のあるほうが，われわれの国防にはいっそう危険です。

　われわれの入念な判断によると，合衆国にとっては無制限に核兵器拡大競争を続けるよりも，部分的でも実験禁止のほうが，はるかに安全な道であります。これらの理由から，わが国が即座に部分的実験禁止条約を承認してくれるものと期待しております。国内でも上院でも，もちろん審議されるでしょう。憲法には，どんな条約を結ぶ時でも上院の勧告と同

wisely requires the advice and consent of the Senate to all treaties, and that consultation has already begun. All this is as it should be. A document which may mark an historic and constructive opportunity for the world deserves an historic and constructive debate. It is my hope that all of you will take part in that debate, for this treaty is for all of us. It is particularly for our children and our grandchildren, and they have no lobby here in Washington. This debate will involve military, scientific, and political experts, but it must not be left to them alone. The right and the responsibility are yours.

If we are to open new doorways to peace, if we are to seize this rare opportunity for progress, if we are to be as bold and farsighted in our control of weapons as we have been in their invention, then let us now show all the world, on this side of the wall and the other, that a strong America also stands for peace. There is no cause for complacency.

We have learned in times past that the spirit of one moment or place can be gone in the next. We have been disappointed more than once, and we have no illusions now that there are short cuts on the road to peace. At many points around the globe the Communists are continuing their efforts to exploit weakness and poverty. Their concentration of nuclear and conventional arms must still be deterred.

意が必要であると規定してありますし，すでに諮問は始まっております。万事うまくいっています。世界に対し歴史的，建設的な好機を示すかもしれない条約の文書は，歴史的，建設的な討論に値します。この討論にぜひ参加して下さい。この条約は皆さん全員のためのものなのです。特にわれわれの子孫のためのものなのです。彼らは今議会に陳情団体を持っていません。この討論には，軍事，科学，および政治の専門家が当然参加していますが，彼らだけの手に委ねるわけにはいきません。あなた方には参加する権利も責任もあります。

　新たな平和への道を開き，この将来の発展への稀なる機会をとらえるつもりなら，そして今までの発明品に対してしてきたように，大胆かつ先見の明で武器を統制するのなら，全世界の両側に対し，断固アメリカも平和のために戦うぞ，というところを見せてやりましょう。自己満足に浸っている時ではありません。

　私達は過去何度となく，ある時ある場所での「やるぞ！」という意気込みが，次の瞬間別の場所ではなくなっていることがあり得るということを知っています。がっかりさせられたことも一度や二度ではありません。が，今や平和への近道があるなどとは夢にも思っていません。地球上いたる所で，共産主義者は弱者と貧民を自分達の悪業のために利用しようと努力を続けているからです。彼らの核兵器と通常兵器の武装はさらに阻止されなくてはなりません。

The familiar contest between choice and coercion, the familiar places of danger and conflict are still there, in Cuba, in Southeast Asia, in Berlin, and all around the globe, still requiring all the strength and the vigilance that we can muster. Nothing could more greatly damage our cause than if we and our allies were to believe that peace has already been achieved and that our strength and unity were no longer required.

But now for the first time in many years the path of peace may be open. No one can be certain what the future will bring. No one can say whether the time has come for an easing of the struggle. But history and our own conscience will judge us harsher if we do not now make every effort to test our hopes by action, and this is the place to begin. According to the ancient Chinese proverb, "A journey of a thousand miles must begin with a single step."

My fellow Americans, let us take that first step. Let us, if we can, get back from the shadows of war and seek out the way of peace. And if that journey is one thousand miles or even more, let history record that we, in this land, at this time, took the first step.

Thank you and good night.

選択か強制かという相変わらずの抗争と，相変わらず危険と紛争に満ちた場所はまだキューバ，東南アジア，ベルリンほか地球上いたる所にあります。だからできる限りの戦力を集中させ，警戒をおこたらないようにする必要があります。われわれと同盟国が，平和はすでに達成され，軍備も同盟ももはや必要なしと考えるようになったら，その時がいちばん，われわれの主義が危い時でしょう。

　しかし今，久し振りに平和への道が開けている時かもしれません。将来はどうなるのか，われわれの苦闘を少しでも楽にしてくれる時が来ているのかどうか誰にもわかりません。しかし，今ここで実際に行動してみて希望がかなうのかどうか試すのに全精力を傾けなければ，われわれは歴史的にも，自分達の良識に照らし合わせてみても厳しく非難を受けるでしょう。この場から始めるべきです。中国のことわざにもあります。

「千里の道も一歩から」です。

　アメリカの皆さん。第一歩を踏み出しましょう。できるなら戦争の脅威から離れて，平和への道を探しましょう。たとえ，それが千里の道程であれ，それ以上であれ，歴史上にわれわれがこの場所で，この瞬間に第一歩を踏み出したということを残そうではありませんか。

　御清聴どうもありがとうございました。

BUILDING THE PEACE

I

Mr. President, Mr. Secretary-General, delegates to the United Nations, Ladies and Gentlemen:

We meet again in the quest for peace.

Twenty-four months ago, when I last had the honor of addressing this body, the shadow of fear lay darkly across the world. The freedom of West Berlin was in immediate peril. Agreement on a neutral Laos seemed remote. The mandate of the U.N. in the Congo was under fire. The financial outlook for this organization was in doubt. Dag Hammarskjöld was dead. The doctrine of Troika was being pressed in his place and atmospheric nuclear tests had recently been resumed by the Soviet Union.

Those were anxious days for mankind—and some men wondered aloud whether this organization could survive. But the 16th and 17th General Assemblies achieved not only survival but progress. Rising to its responsibility, the United Nations helped to reduce the tensions and helped to hold back the darkness.

Today the clouds have lifted a little so that new rays of hope can break through. The pressures on

平 和 の 建 設

I

　議長，事務総長，各国代表ならびに御列席の皆様。
　われわれは平和を求めて，ふたたびここで顔を合わせることになりました。
　2年前，私が国連総会で演説する栄誉を与えられました時には，恐怖の影が世界全体を暗くおおっていました。西ベルリンの自由はさし迫った危険にさらされていました。中立ラオスに関しての合意成立への道は遠いかに見えました。コンゴでの国連軍の行動が非難攻撃を受けておりました。国連の財政的見通しは疑問に包まれていました。ダグ・ハマーショルド事務総長が亡くなりました。同氏に代る総長三人制のトロイカ方式への圧力が加っておりました。そして，少し前にソ連が大気圏内核実験を再開していました。
　当時は人類にとって不安な日々でありました。人々のなかには，国連が存続しうるかどうかは疑わしいと，はっきり言うものもありました。しかし，第16回および第17回総会は，単に存続するだけではなく，進歩をもなし遂げました。国連はその責務を果たそうと立ち上がり，緊張を緩和し，暗雲を払いのける助けをしました。
　今日は暗雲が少しばかり晴れ，雲間から新しい希望の光がさし込みうる状態になっています。西ベルリンに対する圧力

West Berlin appear to be temporarily eased. Political unity in the Congo has been largely restored. A neutral coalition in Laos, while still in difficulty, is at least in being. The integrity of the U.N. Secretariat has been reaffirmed. A U.N. Decade of Development is under way. And, for the first time in 17 years of effort, a specific step has been taken to limit the nuclear arms race.

I refer, of course, to the treaty to ban nuclear tests in the atmosphere, outer space and underwater— concluded by the Soviet Union, the United Kingdom and the United States—and already signed by nearly a hundred countries. It has been hailed by people the world over who are thankful to be free from the fears of nuclear fallout, and I am confident that on next Tuesday morning at 10:30 o'clock, it will receive the overwhelming endorsement of the Senate of the United States.

The world has not yet escaped from the darkness. The long shadows of conflict and crisis envelop us still. But we meet today in an atmosphere of rising hope, and at a moment of comparative calm. My presence here is not a sign of crisis but of confidence. I am not here to report on a new threat to the peace or new signs of war. I have come to salute the United Nations and to show the support of the American people for your daily deliberations.

は、一時的に緩和されているように見えます。コンゴにおける政治的統一は大幅に回復されました。ラオスにおける中立連合は、いまなお困難に直面しているものの、少なくとも存在はしています、国連事務局の本来の姿も再確認されてきています。国連の「開発の十年」が進行中であります。そして、17年にわたる努力において初めて、核軍備競争を制限するための具体的な措置がとられました。

　私がいっているのは、もちろん、ソ連、英国および米国によって締結され、すでに百近くの国によって調印された大気圏内、大気圏外および水中における核実験禁止条約のことであります。同条約は、放射性降下物の恐怖から解放されたことに感謝する世界中の人々から歓呼をもって迎えられました。そして私は、来週火曜日（24日）午前十時半、同条約が米上院の圧倒的多数によって承認されることを確信しているのであります。

　世界はまだ暗黒から脱出したわけではありません。紛争と危機の長い影が、いまなおわれわれを包んでおります。しかし、われわれは今日、希望に胸をふくらませる雰囲気の中で、比較的に平穏な時期に顔を合わせました。私がここに出席していることは、危機の兆しではなく、確信の兆しであります。私は、平和に対する新たな脅威あるいは戦争の新たな兆しについて報告するために、ここに来ているのではありません。国連に敬意を表するため、諸君の日々の討議に対する米国民の支持をここに示すために、私は来たのであります。

For the value of this body's work is not dependent on the existence of emergencies—nor can the winning of the peace consist only of dramatic victories. Peace is a daily, a weekly, a monthly process, gradually changing opinions, slowly eroding old barriers, quietly building new structures. And however undramatic the pursuit a peace, that pursuit must go on.

Today we may have reached a pause in the Cold War—but that is not a lasting peace. A test ban treaty is a milestone—but that is not the millennium. We have not been released from our obligations—we have been given an opportunity. And if we fail to make the most of this moment and this momentum —if we convert our new-found hopes and understanding into new walls and weapons of hostility—if this pause in the Cold War leads merely to its renewal and not its end—then the shaming indictment of posterity will rightly point its finger at us all. But if we can stretch this pause into a period of fruitful cooperation—if both sides can now gain new confidence and true experience in concrete collaborations for peace—if we can now be as bold and farsighted in the control of deadly weapons as we have been in their creation—then, surely, this first small step can be the start of a long and fruitful journey.

なぜならば，国連の仕事の価値は，緊急事態が存在するか否かによって決まるものでなく，またただ単に劇的な勝利を積み重ねただけでは平和を獲得することはできません。平和は，いろいろの意見をしだいに変え，古い障害を徐々に切りくずし，新しい機構を静かに築き上げていくという，日ごとの，週ごとの，月ごとの過程であります。平和の追求がいかに地味なものであるにせよ，この追求は続けていかなければならないのです。

　今日われわれは冷戦の休止点に到達したのかもしれません――しかしこれは恒久的な平和ではありません。実験停止条約は一つの里程標ではありますけれども，しかし現実的時代を到来させたものではないのです。われわれは責務を免れたのではなく，一つの機会を与えられたのです。もしわれわれがこの時期とこの勢いを利用しないなら――もしわれわれが新たに見出した希望と理解を，敵対的な新たな障壁と兵器に置きかえるなら――もしこの冷戦の休止が再開に至るだけで，その終息に至らないなら，後世はわれわれすべてを指弾するでありましょう。しかし，もしわれわれがこの休止期間を延長して成果ある協力の時代を出現させうるなら――もし双方の側とも平和に関する具体的協力に新しい確信と真の経験を獲得しうるなら――もしわれわれが破滅的兵器の創造におけると同様，こうした兵器の管理においても大胆かつ先見の明ある措置をとりうるならば――この小さな第一歩が長い実りの多い旅路への出発となりうることは確かなことです。

II

The task of building the peace lies with the leaders of every nation, large and small. For the great powers have no monopoly on conflict or ambition. The Cold War is not the only expression of tension in this world —and the nuclear race is not the only arms race. Even little wars are dangerous in a nuclear world. The long labor of peace is an undertaking for every nation—and in this effort none of us can remain unaligned. To this goal none can be uncommitted.

The reduction of global tension must not be an excuse for the narrow pursuit of self-interest. If the Soviet Union and the United States, with all of their global interests and clashing commitments of ideology, and with nuclear weapons still aimed at each other today, can find areas of common interest and agreement, then surely other nations can do the same— nations caught in regional conflicts, in racial issues, or in the death throes of old colonialism. Chronic disputes which divert precious resources from the needs of the people, or drain the energies of both sides, serve the interests of no one—and the badge of responsibility in the modern world is a willingness to seek peaceful solutions.

It is never too early to try; it is never too late to talk; and it is high time that many disputes on the

II

　平和を確立する任務は，各国の指導者が大小を問わず帯びています。というのは，大国だけが紛争や野心を独り占めにしているわけではないからであります。冷戦だけがこの世界における緊張の唯一の表現であるというわけではない——また核競争だけが唯一の軍備競争ではありません。小さな戦争でさえ核時代の世界では危険なのであります。平和のための長期にわたる努力は，各国がすべきものである——そしてこの努力には，どの国も不参加のままであってはならないのです。この目標に対しては，どの国も無関心であることはできません。

　世界緊張の緩和は，偏狭な自己の利益を追求する口実にしてはなりません。もし米ソ両国が，そのいろいろの世界的利害関係や相対立する思想にもかかわらず，また今日いまだに相手国を標的とする核兵器を保有しているにもかかわらず，共通の利害と合意の領域を見出しうるなら，他の諸国も同様にこれをなしうることは確かであります——地域的紛争や人種問題を抱えている国々も，旧植民地主義の最後の苦しみにあえいでいる国々も，貴重な資源を国民の需要以外のことに向けたり，双方の側のエネルギーを消耗させる慢性的な紛争は誰の利益にもならないのです。平和的解決を求める積極的意思を示すことこそ，現代世界では責任をもつものの印であります。

　試みるのに早すぎるということはありませんし，また話し合うのに遅すぎるということもありません。いまや本総会の

> agenda of this Assembly were taken off the debating schedule and placed on the negotiating table.

III

The fact remains that the United States, as a major nuclear power, has a special responsibility. It is, in fact, a three-fold responsibility—a responsibility to our own citizens—a responsibility to the people of all the world affected by our decisions—and responsibility to the next generation of humanity. We believe the Soviet Union also has these special responsibilities—and that these responsibilities require our two countries to concentrate less on our differences and more on the means of resolving them peacefully. For too long both of us have increased our nuclear stockpiles and our capacity to destroy all life on this planet—human, animal and vegetable—without any corresponding increase in our security.

Our conflicts, to be sure, are real. Our concepts of the world are different. No service is performed by failing to make clear our disagreements. A central difference is the belief of the American people in self-determination for all people.

We believe that the people of Germany and Berlin must be free to reunite their capital and their country.

We believe that the people of Cuba must be free to secure the fruits of the revolution that has been

> 議題とされている幾多の紛争を，もはや討論の段階ではなく，実際の交渉の場に移すべき時であります。

III

　米国が，主要な核国家として，特別の責任をもつという事実は変わりません。実際上，この責任は，われわれ市民に対する責任，われわれの決定によって影響を受ける世界中の人々に対する責任，次の世代の人々に対する責任，の三重の責任から成っております。ソ連もこうした特別の責任をもっていると信じます。そしてこれらの責任は，われわれ両国の相違よりも，それを平和的に解決するための手段を発見することに力を注ぐことを必要としていると思います。あまりにも長い間われわれ両国は，軍事予算と，核兵器貯蔵量と，人間と動植物を含む地上すべての生物を破壊する能力を増強してきましたが，われわれの安全性はそれに応じて強化されてはおりません。

　たしかに，われわれの意見の相違点をはっきりさせることを避けたとして，何の役に立つものでもありません。主要な相違点は，米国民がすべての国民は自決権をもたなければならないと信じていることにあります。

　われわれはドイツ国民とベルリン市民は，その首都とその国家を再統一する自由をもつべきであると信じています。

　われわれはキューバ国民が，国の内外から全く無残に裏切

so falsely betrayed from within and exploited from without.

In short, we believe that in all the world—in Eastern Europe as well as Western, in southern Africa as well as northern, in old nations as well as new—people must be free to choose their own future, without discrimination or dictation, and without coercion or subversion.

These are basic differences between ourselves and the Soviet Union, and they cannot be concealed. So long as they exist, they set limits to agreement, and they forbid the relaxation of vigilance. Our defenses around the world will be maintained for the protection of freedom—and our determination to safeguard that freedom will measure up to any threat or challenge.

But I would say to the leaders of the Soviet Union, and to their people, that if either of our countries is to be fully secure, we need a much better weapon than the H-bomb—a weapon better than ballistic missiles or nuclear submarines—and that better weapon is peaceful cooperation.

We have, in recent years, agreed on a limited nuclear test ban treaty—on an emergency communications link between our capitals—on a statement of principles for disarmament—on an increase in cultural exchange—on cooperation in outer space—on the peaceful exploration of the Antarctic—and on temper-

られた革命の成果を確保する自由をもつべきであると信じています。

　要するに，われわれは，全世界を通じて――西欧と東欧，北アフリカと南アフリカ，新国家と旧国家を含めて――人々は，差別や命令や強制や破壊工作を受けずに，自らの将来を選ぶ自由をもたなければならないと信じております。

　これらが，われわれとソ連との間にある根本的な意見の相違点であって，それをおおい隠すことはできません。こうした相違が存在する以上は，合意にも限界があります。そしてそのために警戒を怠ることが許されないのであります。全世界にわたるわれわれの防衛陣は，自由を護るために維持されるでありましょう。そしてこの自由を護ろうとするわれわれの決意は，いかなる脅かし，挑戦にも耐え得るでありましょう。

　しかし私は，ソ連の指導者と国民に対して言いたいのです。もし両国が十分に安全でいるためには，われわれは，水素爆弾よりもはるかにすぐれた武器，弾頭ミサイルや原子力潜水艦よりもすぐれた武器が必要なのであります。そしてこのすぐれた武器とは平和的協力にほかならないのです。

　われわれは近年，部分的核実験停止条約において，両国首都間の緊急用通信線設定において，軍縮に関する原則の声明において，文化交換の促進において，大気圏外での協力において，南極圏の平和的探検において，また昨年度のキューバ

ing last year's crisis over Cuba.

IV

I believe, therefore, that the Soviet Union and the United States, together with their allies, can achieve further agreements—agreements which spring from our mutual interest in avoiding mutual destruction.

There can be no doubt about the agenda of further steps. We must continue to seek agreement on measures to prevent war by accident or miscalculation. We must continue to seek agreement on safeguards against surprise attack, including observation posts at key points. We must continue to seek agreement on further measures to curb the nuclear arms race, by controlling the transfer of nuclear weapons, converting fissionable materials to peaceful purposes, and banning underground testing with adequate inspection and enforcement. We must continue to seek agreement on a freer flow of information and people from East to West and West to East.

We must continue to seek agreement, encouraged by yesterday's affirmative response to this proposal by the Soviet Foreign Minister, on an arrangement to keep weapons of mass destruction out of outer space. Let us get our negotiators back to the negotiating table to work out a practicable arrangement to this end.

危機克服において，合意に達してきました。

IV

　したがって，ソ連と米国は，双方の同盟諸国をも含めて，さらにいろいろな協定——相互破壊の回避にわれわれがお互いに関心を持っていることから生まれる協定——を達成し得ると，私は信じております。

　今後の措置として取り上げるべきことがらについては，なんらの疑問もありえません。われわれは引き続き，偶然や誤算による戦争を防止するための措置について合意の達成に努力しなければなりません。主要地点への監視所設置など，奇襲攻撃防止のための措置について，合意の達成に努力しなければなりません。核兵器譲渡の規制核分裂物質の平和目的への転換，適切な査察・実施制度を伴った地下実験禁止など，核軍備競争抑制のため今後さらにとるべき措置について合意の達成に努力しなければなりません。また，東から西へ，西から東への情報および人々の交流自由化について，合意の達成に努力しなければならないのです。

　われわれは，きのうソ連外相がこの提案に対して肯定的な反応を示したことに勇気づけられて，大量破壊兵器を大気圏外に送り込まないという取り決めについて合意を求めつづけなければなりません。われわれは，この目的のための実行可能な取り決めを定めるために，われわれの交渉代表を交渉の席に戻らせようではありませんか。

In these and other ways, let us move up the steep and difficult path toward comprehensive disarmament, securing mutual confidence through mutual verification, and building the institutions of peace as we dismantle the engines of war. We must not let failure to agree on all points delay agreement where agreement is possible. And we must not put forward proposals merely for propaganda purposes.

Finally, in a field where the United States and the Soviet Union have a special capacity—the field of space—there is room for new cooperation for further joint efforts in the regulation and exploration of space. It includes among these possibilities a joint expedition to the moon. Space offers no problem of sovereignty; by resolution of this Assembly, the members of the United Nations have forsworn any claims to territorial rights in outer space or on celestial bodies, and declared that international law and the U.N. Charter will apply. Why, therefore, should man's first flight to the moon be a matter of national competition? Why should the United States and the Soviet Union, in preparing for such expeditions, become involved in immense duplications of research, construction and expenditure? Surely we should explore whether the scientists and astronauts of our two countries—indeed of all the world—cannot work together in the conquest of space, sending some day of this decade to

これらの方法およびその他の方法で，相互的検証によって相互的信頼を確保しながら，また戦争の道具を解体するにつれて平和の諸制度を築きながら，包括的な軍縮への，けわしく困難な道を登って行こうではありませんか。あらゆる点について合意することが出来ないからといって，合意の可能な領域での合意成立を遅らせることがあってはなりません。また，単に宣伝目的のためだけに提案を出すべきではありません。

　最後に，米国とソ連が特別の能力をもつ分野——宇宙の分野——では，宇宙の規制と探査の面で，さらに共同の努力を払うため，両国が新たに協力する余地があります。これらの可能性の中に，月への共同探検を含めようではありませんか。宇宙にはどの国が主権をとるかという問題はありません。国連加盟国はこの総会の決議によって，大気圏外または天体における領土権の主張をしないことを誓い，国際法と国連憲章を適用することを宣言しました。それなのに月への人間の最初の飛行がなぜ国家的な競争の問題とならなければならないのでしょうか。また米国とソ連はなぜこのような探検の準備のため，研究，建設，および経費の点でぼう大な重複をおかすようなことをしなければならないのでしょうか。われわれは，両国——いな全世界——の科学者と宇宙航空士が，60年代のいつか，一国の代表者だけでなくすべての人類の代表者

the moon, not the representatives of a single nation, but the representatives of all humanity.

All these and other new steps toward peaceful cooperation may be possible. Most of them will require on our part full consultation with our allies—for their interests are as much involved as our own, and we will never make an agreement at their expense.

Most of them will require long and careful negotiations. And most of them will require a new approach to the Cold War—a desire not to "bury" one's adversary but to compete in a host of peaceful arenas, in ideas, in production, and in service to all humanity.

The contest will continue—the contest between those who envision a monolithic world and those who believe in diversity—but it should be a contest in leadership instead of intimidation. Speaking for the United States of America, I welcome such a contest. For we believe that truth is stronger than error—and that freedom is more enduring than coercion. And in the contest for a better life, all the world can be the winner.

V

The effort to improve the conditions of man, however, is not the task of a few. It is the task of all nations—acting alone, acting in groups, and acting in the United Nations. For plague and pestilence, plun-

を月に送り，宇宙を征服することに協力できないかどうか検討すべきです。

平和的な協力のためのこれらおよびほかの新しい措置は可能であると思われます。その大部分は，われわれが同盟諸国と十分協議する必要があるでしょう——なぜなら彼らの利害もわれわれと同じくらい深い関係があるからであり，われわれは彼らの犠牲において協定を結ぶつもりは全くないからであります。

またその大部分は，長期にわたる慎重な交渉を必要とするでありましょう。また，その大部分は，冷戦への新たな態度——敵を「葬むる」ことを望むのではなくて，思想，生産，全人類への奉仕といった多くの平和的な分野で競争しようという願望——を必要とするでありましょう。

一元的な世界をもくろむ者たちと，多様性を信じる者の間の競争は続くでしょうが，しかしそれは破壊ではなくて指導力，脅迫ではなくて成果での競争でなければなりません。私はアメリカ合衆国を代表して，こうした競争を歓迎するものです。なぜなら，真実が誤ちよりも強く，自由が強制よりも永続的なものであることをわれわれは信じているからです。そしてよりよい生活を求める競争では，世界全体が勝利となりうるのであります。

V

しかし，人間の生活条件を改善するための努力は，少数の国の仕事ではありません。それは単独で行動するか，集団で行動するか，また国連において行動するかなどを問わず，あらゆる国家の仕事であります。なぜなら，伝染病や流行病，

der and pollution, the hazards of nature and the hunger of children are the foes of every nation. The earth, the sea, and the air are the concern of every nation. And science, technology and education can be the allies of every nation.

Never before has man had such capacity to control his own environment—to end thirst and hunger—to conquer poverty and disease—to banish illiteracy and massive human misery. We have the power to make this the best generation of mankind in the history of the world—or to make it the last.

The United States since the close of the war has sent over $100 billion worth of assistance to nations seeking economic viability. And two years ago this week we formed a Peace Corps to help interested countries meet their needs for trained and inspired manpower. Other industrialized nations—whose economies were rebuilt not so long ago with our help—are now in turn recognizing their responsibility to the less-developed nations.

The provision of development assistance by individual nations must go on. But the United Nations also must play a larger role in helping bring to all men the fruits of modern science and industry. A U.N. conference on this subject, held earlier this year in Geneva, opened new vistas for the developing nations. Next year a U.N. conference on trade will

資源の強奪や環境の汚染，天災や子供たちの飢えといったものは，各国民の敵だからです。大地と海洋と空間にはどの国家も関心をもっています。そして科学と技術と教育は，すべての国家の味方となることができるのであります。

　人類が，渇きと飢えをなくし，貧困と病気にうちかち，文盲と重苦しい人間の不幸を消し去り，自分自身の環境を制御するこのような能力をもったことはかつてありませんでした。われわれは今の世代を世界歴史上，人類の最良の世代とするか，あるいはこれを最後のものとする力をもっております。

　第二次世界大戦の終結以来，米国は経済的自活力を求めている国々に対して，一千億ドル余の援助を与えてきました。そして2年前の今週，われわれは関係諸国が訓練され，啓発された人的資源の必要を満たすのを助けるために，平和部隊を組織しました。あまり遠くない過去にわれわれの援助によって経済を再建した諸国も，いまや低開発諸国に対する責任を認識しつつあります。

　個々の国による開発援助の供与は続けられなければなりません。しかし，国連もまた，近代的科学および産業の成果をすべての人々にもたらすことに，より大きな役割を果たさなければなりません。今年ジュネーブで開かれたこの問題についての国連会議は，新興諸国に新たな将来への希望を与えました。来年の国連貿易会議では，新しい市場に対するこれら

consider the needs of these nations for new markets. And more than four-fifths of the entire United Nations system can be found today mobilizing the weapons of science and technology for the U.N.'s decade of development.

But more, much more, can be done. For example:

—A world center for health communications under the World Health Organization could warn of epidemics and of the adverse effects of certain drugs as well as transmit the results of new experiments and new discoveries.

—Regional research centers could advance our common medical knowledge and train new scientists and doctors for new nations.

—A global system of satellites could provide communication and weather information for all corners of the earth.

—A world-wide program of conservation could protect the forest and wild game preserves now in danger of extinction.

—Improve the marine harvest of food from our oceans—and prevent the contamination of our air and our water by industrial as well as nuclear pollution.

—And, finally, a world-wide program of farm productivity and food distribution—similar to my own nation's "Food for Peace" program—could give every hungry child the food he needs.

の新興諸国の必要が検討されることになっています。また，国連全加盟国の五分の四以上が今日，科学と技術のもろもろの武器を，国連の「開発の十年」のために動員していることが認められます。

　しかし，もっと多くのこと，はるかに多くのことを行なうことができます。たとえば，──世界保健機構のもとに世界保健通信センターを設ければ，伝染病について警告したり，ある種の薬剤の有害な影響について警告したり，新しい実験や新発見の成果を伝えたりすることができるのです。

　──地域研究センターを設ければ，医学に関する知識を向上させ，新興諸国のために新しい科学者や医師を養成することができます。

　──全世界的人工衛星網を設定すれば，世界の隅々に通信や気象情報をいきわたらせることができるのです。

　──世界的資源保存計画を実施すれば，現在，絶滅の危機に瀕している森林資源や野性動物を保護し，海洋から食糧の採取を増やし，工場や原子力施設などによる大気や水の汚染を防止することができるのです。

　──そして最後に，世界農業生産性・食糧配給計画──米国の「平和のための食糧」計画に似通った計画──を実施すれば，すべての空腹な子供にその必要とする食糧を与えることができるのです。

VI

But man does not live by bread alone—and the members of this organization are committed by the Charter to promote and respect human rights. Those rights are not respected when a Buddhist priest is driven from his pagoda, when a synagogue is shut down, when a Protestant church cannot open a mission, when a cardinal is forced into hiding, or when a crowded church service is bombed.

The United States of America is opposed to discrimination and persecution on grounds of race and religion anywhere in the world, including our own nation. We are working to right the wrongs of our own nation.

Through legislation and administrative action, through moral and legal commitment, this Government has launched a determined effort to rid our nation of discrimination which has existed far too long—in education, in housing, in transportation, in employment, in the civil service, in recreation, and in places of public accommodation. And therefore, in this or in any other forum, we do not hesitate to condemn racial or religious injustice, whether committed or permitted by friends or by foes.

I know that some of you have experienced discrimination in this country. But I ask you to believe

VI

　しかし人はパンだけで生きるものではありません。そして国連加盟諸国は，憲章によって人権を増進し尊重することを委託されています。仏教僧が寺院から追い出されたり，ユダヤ教会堂が閉鎖されたり，プロテスタント教会が布教本部を設けることができなかったり，枢機卿が身を隠さなければならなかったり，人がいっぱいの礼拝式に爆弾がしかけられたりしたのでは，これらの権利が尊重されているとはいえません。

　米国は自国をはじめ世界のどの地域にせよ，人種的・宗教的理由による差別や迫害に反対しています。われわれはわが国内の誤まった行為をただすように努めています。

　米国政府は，立法措置と行政措置によって，道義的公約と法的公約を通じて，これまでにあまりにも長く続いてきた教育，住宅，交通，雇用，公務員任用，レクリエーション，公共施設における人種差別等を米国から一掃しようと，決然たる努力を開始しています。したがって，われわれは，この議場あるいはその他のいかなる討論の場においても，人種上または宗教上の不公正が行なわれたり，容認されている場合，それが味方であろうと，敵であろうとこれを非難するのに躊躇しません。

　あなた方の中には，米国で人種差別を経験された方もあると思います。でも，これは大部分のアメリカ人の意思による

me when I tell you that this is not the wish of most Americans—that we share your regret and resentment—and that we intend to end such practices for all time to come, not only for our visitors but for all our citizens as well.

I hope that not only our nation but all other multiracial societies will meet these standards of fairness and justice. We are opposed to apartheid and all forms of human oppression. We do not advocate the rights of black Africans in order to drive out white Africans. Our concern is the right of all men to equal protection under the law—and since human rights are indivisible, this body cannot stand aside when those rights are abused or neglected by any member state.

New efforts are needed if this Assembly's Declaration of Human Rights, now 15 years old, is to have full meaning. And new means should be found for promoting the free expression and trade of ideas—through better travel and communications, and through increased exchanges of people, books and broadcasts. For as the world renounces the competition of weapons, competition in ideas must flourish—and the competition must be as full and fair as possible.

VII

The United States delegation will be prepared to

ものではなく，またわれわれも同様の遺憾の念と怒りを感じるものであり，またこうした慣行をわが国に来る人々のためだけでなく，全米国民のためにも，永久になくしたいと思っていることを私はここにはっきり断言いたします。

　私は，わが国ばかりでなく，すべての多民族国家が公正で正義を伴ったこうした基準を守ることを希望します。われわれは人種差別政策とあらゆる形の人間圧迫に，断固として反対します。われわれは，アフリカの白人を追い出すためにアフリカの黒人の権利を主張するものではありません。われわれの関心はすべての人間が平等の保護と希望ある機会をもつ権利を得ることにあります。そして人権は切りはなすことのできないものですから，この権利が国連に加盟しているどこかの一国によって悪用されたり無視されたりした場合には，国連は傍観していることはできないのであります。

　国連総会が人権宣言を発してから15年になりますが，その人権宣言が完全に意味をもつようにするには新たな努力が必要です。そして，表現の自由と思想の交流を促進するために，旅行と通信の便をよくし，人々や書物や放送の交流を盛んにするなど新たな手段が見出されなくてはなりません。なぜなら世界の武器の競争を放棄するにつれて，思想の競争を盛んにしなくてはならないし，この競争はできる限り全面的で公平なものでなくてはならないからであります。

Ⅶ

　米国代表は，いま私が述べた目標のすべてを追求する上で，

suggest U.N. initiatives in pursuit of all the goals I have mentioned, for this is an organization for peace —and peace cannot come without progress.

The peacekeeping record of the United Nations has been a proud one, though its tasks are always formidable. We are fortunate to have the skills of our distinguished Secretary-General and the brave efforts of those who have been serving the cause of peace in the Congo and the Middle East, in Korea and the Kashmir, in West New Guinea and Malaysia. But what the U.N. has done in the past is less important than its task for the future. We cannot take its peacekeeping machinery for granted. That machinery must be soundly financed—which it cannot be if some members are allowed to prevent it from meeting its obligations by failing to meet their own. The United Nations must be supported by all who exercise their franchise here. And its operations must be backed to the end.

Too often, a project undertaken in the excitement of crisis begins to lose its appeal as the problems drag on and the bills pile up. But we must have the steadfastness to see each enterprise through.

It is, for example, most important not to jeopardize the extraordinary U.N. gains in the Congo. The nation which sought this organization's help only three years ago has now asked the U.N. presence to remain

国連がイニシアチブをとるよう提案する構えがあります。それは国連が平和のための機構であり，平和は進歩なくしてはやって来ないからであります。

　国連の仕事は常に手ごわいものばかりですが，その平和維持の記録は，誇ってよいものです。そして幸いなことに，卓越した事務総長の手腕と，コンゴや中東，韓国やカシミール，西ニューギニアやマレーシアで平和を実現するために努めた人々の勇敢な努力があります。しかし国連がこれまで行なってきたことより，将来の仕事の方がずっと重要です。われわれはその平和維持機構を，それでよいことにしているわけにはいきません。この機構の財政を，健全にしなくてはなりません。それは，加盟国のうちに自己の負担金を払わぬことによって，この機構の義務履行を妨げることが許されるようであってはできないのです。国連はこの総会で投票権を行使するすべてのものに支持されなくてはなりません。国連の作業は究極まで後押しされるべきであります。

　危機の興奮のうちに企てられた計画が，問題が長びき，経費がかさんでくるにつれて，人に訴える力を失いはじめる例はあまりにも多い。しかしわれわれはおのおのの企てを最後まで見守る堅実さを持たなければなりません。

　たとえば，国連がコンゴで挙げた大成功をそこなわないようにすることが，もっとも大切であります。わずか三年前，国連の援助を頼んだこの国は，いまや国連がもう少し長く同

a little longer. I believe this Assembly should do what is necessary to preserve the gains already made and to protect the new nation in its struggle for progress. Let us complete what we've started, for "no man who puts his hand to the plow and looks back," as the scriptures tell us, "no man who puts his hand to the plow and looks back, is fit for the kingdom of God."

I also hope that the recent initiative of several members in preparing standby peace forces for United Nations call will encourage similar commitments by others. This nation remains ready to provide logistic and other material support.

Policing, moreover, is not enough without provision for pacific settlement. We should increase the resort to special missions of fact-finding and conciliation, make greater use of the International Court of Justice, and accelerate the work of the International Law Commission.

The United Nations cannot survive as a static organization. Its obligations are increasing as well as its size. Its charter must be changed as well as its customs. The authors of that charter did not intend that it be frozen in perpetuity. The science of weapons and war has made us all, far more than eighteen years ago in San Francisco, one world and one human race with one common destiny.

国に留まることを要請しています。私は本総会は、すでに収めた成功を維持し、自国の進歩のために闘うこの新国家を保護するため、あらゆる必要なことをすべきだと考えます。われわれがはじめたことは、われわれが完成しようではありませんか。聖書にもありますように、「手をすきにかけてからうしろを見る者は、神の国にふさわしくないものである」

最近、加盟国数ヵ国が率先して国連の求めに応じられる平和維持兵力を待機させることに至りましたが、これが他国を元気づけて同様の措置をとらせることを私は望んでいます。米国は兵たんその他の物質的援助を提供する用意をつねに整えております。

そのうえ、治安の維持は平和的解決の規定を欠いては十分ではありません。われわれは実情調査と調停の両特別使節団をより多く活用し、国際司法裁判所をもっと多く利用し、そして国際法委員会の仕事を促進すべきであります。

国連は、静止した機構として存続してゆくことはできません。規模と同様、責任も増大しているのです。慣習と同様、憲章も改定されなければなりません。国連憲章の起草者たちは、憲章を永久に凍結してしまおうとは考えていなかったのです。兵器と戦争の科学はサンフランシスコの18年前に比べてはるかに大きく、一つの運命を分かち合った一つの世界、一つの人類の方向へわれわれすべてを進ませたのです。

このような世界では、絶対的主権はもはやわれわれに絶対的な安全を保証しません。平和のためのものが戦争のための

In such a world, absolute sovereignty no longer assures us of absolute security. The conventions of peace must pull abreast and then ahead of the inventions of war. The United Nations, building on its successes and learning from its failures, must be developed into a genuine world security system.

VIII

But peace does not rest in the charters and covenants alone. It lies in the hearts and minds of all people. And if in this world out here no act, no pact, no treaty or organization can ever hope to preserve it without the support and the whole-hearted commitment of all people. So let us not rest all our hopes on parchment and on paper—let us strive to build peace—a desire for peace, a willingness to work for peace—in the hearts and minds of our people.

I believe that we can. I believe the problems of human destiny are not beyond the reach of human beings.

Two years ago I told this body that the United States had proposed, and was willing to sign, a limited test ban treaty. Today that treaty has been signed. It will not put an end to war. It will not remove basic conflicts. It will not secure freedom for all. But it can be a lever. And Archimedes, in explaining the principles of the lever, was said to have declared to

ものに追いつき，さらにこれを追い越すようにならなければなりません。国連は成功したことを土台にして伸び，失敗を教訓として，真の世界安全保障機構にまで発展させられなければならないのです。

Ⅷ

　しかし，平和は憲章や盟約だけに根ざすものではありません。それはすべての人々の心情のなかに根ざすものであり，この世の中で，どんな行動，どんな協約，どんな条約ないし機構によっても，すべての人々の支援と心からの参加なしにこれを維持することは望めません。ですから，平和に対するわれわれの希望を文書だけに託するのではなく，人々の心情のなかに──平和の欲求，平和への進んでの努力──平和を築きあげることにも努力しようではありませんか。

　われわれはそうすることができると思います。人間の運命の問題は人類が解決しえないものではないと思うのです。

　2年前，本総会において，私は米国が部分的核実験停止条約を提案し，これに調印する用意があると述べました。今日この条約は調印を終わりました。それは，戦争を終わらせはしないでありましょう。また根本的な相違を取り除きはしないでしょう。すべてのものの自由を保証はしないでありましょう。だが一つのテコにはなり得ます。アルキメデスはテコの原理を友人に説明して，こう言ったそうです。「私が立っていられる足場を与えてくれないか。そうすれば世界を動かして見せよう」と。

　この地球にともに住む諸君よ。この各国の集会場を，われわれの足場にしようではありませんか。そしてわれわれの時代

his friends: "Give me a place where I can stand—and I shall move the world."

My fellow inhabitants of this planet: Let us take our stand here in this assembly of nations. And let us see if we, in our time, can move the world toward just and lasting peace.

に，この世界を正しい永続的な平和に向かって動かせるかどうかやって見ようではありませんか。

WE WILL CARRY ON

Mr. Speaker, Mr. President, members of the House, members of Senate, my fellow Americans:

All I have I would have given gladly not to be standing here today.

The greatest leader of our time has been struck down by the foulest deed of our time. Today John Fitzgerald Kennedy lives on in the immortal words and works that he left behind. He lives on in the mind and memories of mankind. He lives on in the hearts of his countrymen.

No words are sad enough to express our sense of loss. No words are strong enough to express our determination to continue the forward thrust of America that he began.

The dream of conquering the vastness of space—the dream of partnership across the Atlantic—and across the Pacific as well—the dream of a Peace Corps in less-developed nations—the dream of education for all of our children—the dream of jobs for all who seek them and need them—the dream of care for our elderly—the dream of an all-out attack on mental illness—and above all, the dream of equal rights for

続けようではありませんか

　皆さん，

　今日この壇上に立つにあたってまことに万感胸に迫る思いがするのであります。

　われわれの時代の最も違大なる指導者が，最も憎むべき行為のためになくなりました。しかし今日でもジョン・F・ケネディ大統領は，われわれに残してくれた永遠に不滅の言葉や業績の中に生き続けています。

　彼を失った気持ちがどんなに悲しいことかはどんな言葉でも言いつくせません。彼が始めてくれたアメリカの力強い前進をこれからわれわれが引き継ごうという決意がどんなに強いものか，やはり言葉では言い尽くせません。

　広大な宇宙を征服しようという夢，大西洋はもちろん太平洋を越えて協力し合うという夢，開発途上国に平和部隊を設ける夢，われわれの子孫全員に教育を受けさせようという夢，仕事を探し，必要としている人全員に仕事を与えようという夢，老人をいたわろうという夢，精神病を完治させようとする夢，その中でも特に国籍，人種によらずすべてのアメリカ

all Americans, whatever their race or color—these and other American dreams have been vitalized by his drive and by his dedication.

And now the ideas and the ideals which he so nobly represented must and will be translated into effective action.

Under John Kennedy's leadership, this nation has demonstrated that it has the courage to seek peace, and it has the fortitude to risk war. We have proved that we are a good and reliable friend to those who seek peace and freedom. We have shown that we can also be a formidable foe to those who reject the path of peace and seek to impose upon us or our allies the yoke of tyranny.

This nation will keep its commitments from South Vietnam to West Berlin. We will be unceasing in the search for peace; resourceful in our pursuit of areas of agreement even with those with whom we differ; and generous and loyal to those who join with us in common cause.

In this age where there can be no losers in peace and no victors in war, we must recognize the obligation to match national strength with national restraint. We must be prepared at one and the same time for both the confrontation of power and the limitation of power. We must be ready to defend the national interest and to negotiate the common interest. This is the path that we shall continue to pursue. Those

人に平等の権利をという夢や他のアメリカの夢は，彼の積極的な努力と献身により活気に満ちたものとなりました。

今こそ，彼が堂々と示してくれた思想と理想は効果的に実行に移されなければなりません。

ケネディ大統領の指揮のもと，わが国は進んで平和を求め戦争が起こりそうになっても，がまん強く辛抱する勇気があることを世界中に示しています。われわれは平和と自由を求める国にとっては頼りになるよき味方であり，平和への道を閉ざし，われわれおよび同盟国に対し専制政治を押しつけようとする国にとっては，恐るべき敵になり得ることを示しています。

わが国は南ベトナムからベルリンまで責務を遂行し続けるでしょう。われわれは平和への道を探すことを止めません。われわれと考え方が違う国々とさえ，少しでも同意を得ようと努力し続けるでしょうし，共通の目的でわれわれに加わる国々に対しては寛大で誠意を示すでしょう。

平和でいても敗者がなく戦争をやっても勝者がいない，ということがあり得るこの時代だから，国家の力と国家の自制力とを釣り合わせる義務があることを認識する必要があります。われわれは軍事力を制限することと，お互いの力を比較し釣り合わせることの2つを同時にする覚悟ができていなければなりません。各国の利益は進んで守り，共通の利益については話し合わなければなりません。これこそわれわれが追求し続けようとしていることなのです。われわれの勇気が本

who test our courage will find it strong, and those who seek our friendship will find it honorable. We will demonstrate anew that the strong can be just in the use of strength; and the just can be strong in the defense of justice.

And let all know that we will extend no special privilege and impose no persecution. We will carry on the fight against poverty and misery, and disease and ignorance, in other lands and in our own.

We will serve all of the nation, not one section or one sector, or one group, but all Americans.

These are the United States—a united people with a united purpose.

Our American unity does not depend upon unanimity. We have differences; but now, as in the past, we can derive from those differences strength, not weakness; wisdom, not despair. Both as a people and as a government, we can unite upon a program which is wise, just, enlightened, and constructive.

For thirty-two years, Capitol Hill has been my home. I have shared many moments of pride with you—pride in the ability of the Congress of the United States to act; to meet any crisis; to distill from our differences strong programs of national action.

An assassin's bullet has thrust upon me the awesome burden of the Presidency. I am here today to say that I need your help; I cannot bear this burden

物かどうかを試されることがあっても，結局は本物であることがわかるでしょう。われわれに友情を求める国々はわれわれが信用に値するということがわかるでしょう。強いものが正しい時に力をふるい，正しい者は正義を守るときには強くなり得るということをわれわれは新たに世界に示します。

そしてわれわれは何の特権も拡大せず，迫害もしないということを全世界に知らしめましょう。われわれは他国であれ，自国内であれ，貧乏な人をなくし，不幸な人を助け，病気をなくし，無知をなくすために戦い続けます。

われわれは国民全体に貢献するのです。ある階級，ある分野，ある集団にではなく全アメリカ人に対してです。

いろいろな人が集まってできた国，それがアメリカなのです。一つの目的で結ばれた一つの国民なのです。

でも，このアメリカが一つに結ばれているのは，皆が同じ意見であるからではありません。われわれは皆違うのです。しかし今回も，今までと同じように，この相違点から弱点ではなく，長所を引き出すことができます。一国民としてと同時に一政府として，賢明で，正しい，啓発された，建設的な計画のもとで一致協力できます。

この32年間，連邦議事堂は私にとっていわばわが家でありました。私は皆さんと多くの誇りに思う時間を分かち合ってきました。それらはわが合衆国議会が議決することができたという誇りや，いろいろな危機に直面しましたが，それらを打開したという誇りや，われわれは全員意見が違うにもかかわらずその中から国家的運動の強力な計画を作ったという誇り等です。

暗殺者の弾丸により指導者を失ったため，私は今ここで大統領という大役をになうことになりました。それで今日ここに皆さんの御支援をお願いしに参りました。私は独りではこ

alone. I need the help of all Americans, and all America. This nation has experienced a profound shock, and in this critical moment it is our duty, yours and mine, as the Government of the United States, to do away with uncertainty and to show that we are capable of decisive action; that from the brutal loss of our leader we will derive not weakness but strength; that we can and will act, and act now.

From this chamber of representative government let all the world know, and none misunderstand, that I rededicate this Government to the unswerving support of the United Nations—to the honorable and determined execution of our commitments to our allies—to the maintenance of military strength second to none—to the defense of the strength and stability of the dollar—to the expansion of our foreign trade—to the re-enforcement of our programs of mutual assistance and cooperation in Asia and Africa—and to our Alliance for Progress in this hemisphere.

On the twentieth of January, in 1961, John F. Kennedy told his countrymen that our national work would not be finished "in the first one thousand days, nor in the life of this Administration, nor even perhaps in our lifetime on this planet. But," he said, "let us begin."

Today in this moment of new resolve, I would say to my fellow Americans, let us continue.

の大役の重荷に耐えかねます。すべてのアメリカ人，アメリカ全体の援助をお願いしたいのです。わが国は深い悲しみにつつまれています。そして今この重大な局面にあって，この不安定な状況を取り除くこと，およびわれわれは決定的な行動がとれるのだ，われわれは指導者を失ったからといって弱くなるのではなく，逆に強くなるのだ，そして今行動に移す能力も意志もあるのだ，ということを示すのがわれわれの，あなた方の，そして私の義務です。

　議会制政治のこの議院から全世界に，以下のようなことをわれわれがやろうとしているのだと知らしめ，誤解されないようにしましょう。われわれは国連に確固たる支援を送ります。そして同盟国に対し忠実に一生懸命任務を遂行します。他にひけをとらない軍事力を保持し続けます。ドルの力と安定を守ります。対外貿易を拡張します。アジアとアフリカにおける相互援助と強力計画を強化します。西半球の進歩のための同盟を強化しますと。

　1961年の1月20日にケネディ大統領は国民に，「われわれの国家をあげての仕事は1000日かかっても，この政府が続いている間でも，ひょっとしたら生涯かかっても終わらないかもしれませんが。が，とにかく始めましょう」と言いました。

　今日，新たな決意をしたこの瞬間にみなさんに言いたいのです。さあ続けましょうと。

This is our challenge—not to hesitate, not to pause, not to turn about and linger over this evil moment, but to continue on our course so that we may fulfill the destiny that history has set for us. Our most immediate tasks are here on this Hill.

First, no memorial oration or eulogy could more eloquently honor President Kennedy's memory than the earliest possible passage of the Civil Rights Bill for which he fought. We have talked long enough in this country about equal rights. We have talked for 100 years or more. Yes, it is time now to write the next chapter—and to write it in the books of law.

I urge you again, as I did in 1957, and again in 1960, to enact a civil rights law so that we can move forward to eliminate from this nation every trace of discrimination and oppression based upon race or color. There could be no greater source of strength to this nation both at home and abroad.

And second, no act of ours could more fittingly continue the work of President Kennedy than the earliest passage of the Tax Bill for which he fought all this long year. This is a bill designed to increase our national income and federal revenues, and to provide insurance against recession. That bill, if passed without delay, means more security for those now working, more jobs for those now without them, and more incentive for our economy.

これはわれわれの挑戦です。ためらわないで，時間をおかないで，この邪悪なときにとどまらず，歴史がわれわれに用意した運命に従うためにわが道を進み続けるのです。われわれが今しなければならないことは，ここ国会議事堂にあるのです。

　第一にケネディ大統領が獲得しようとして戦った公民権法案を，ごく早い時期に可決することほど，彼についての思い出をたたえる記念演説は他にあり得ないでしょう。われわれは充分に長い間平等権の必要性について話し続けてきました。100年以上もです。そうです。今こそ次なる章を書く時です。そして法律に書き加えましょう。

　1957年と，1960年に再度皆さんを促したようにもう一度お願いします。市民権を制定し，この国から人権や肌の色によって差別や弾圧されることを排除する方向に進みましょう。この国にとってそれ以上の力の源となるものは国内外において他にないでしょう。

　第二に，長年にわたって戦ってきた税制法案を可決することほど，彼の仕事を適切に続けていくであろう法案は他にないでしょう。この法案は国家収入と連邦の歳入を増やさせ，不景気の時に備えるものです。この法案は順調に議会を通過すれば，今，働いている人達にもっと多くの保障を与え，失業中の人々にもっと仕事を与え，経済に刺激を与えることになります。

In short, this is no time for delay. It is a time for action—strong, forward-looking action on the pending education bills to help bring the light of learning to every home and hamlet in America—strong, forward-looking action on youth employment opportunities, strong forward-looking action on the pending Foreign Aid Bill, making clear that we are not forfeiting our responsibilities to this hemisphere or to the world, nor erasing executive flexibility in the conduct of foreign affairs—and strong, prompt and forward-looking action on the remaining appropriation bills.

In this new spirit of action the Congress can expect the full cooperation and support of the Executive Branch. And in particular, I pledge that the expenditures of your Government will be administered with the utmost thrift and frugality. I will insist that the Government get a dollar's value for a dollar spent. The Government will set an example of prudence and economy. This does not mean we will not meet our unfilled needs, nor that we will not honor our commitments. We will do both.

As one who has long served in both houses of the Congress, I firmly believe in the independence and integrity of the Legislative Branch, and I promise you that I shall always respect this. It is deep in the marrow of my bones. With equal firmness, I believe in the capacity and the ability of the Congress, despite

手短に言えば，ぐずぐずしているときではないのです。行動に移すときなのです。学問の光をアメリカのどの家庭にも，どんな小さな村にまでも投げかけてくれると期待される，かねてから懸案の教育法案についての力強い前向きの行動と，若者を職につかせる機会を与える行動をとるべき時です。われわれは，西半球や世界に対する責任を放棄しつつあるのではなく，外交問題を指導する際に大統領の融通性をなくしてもいないということを明らかにし，懸案だった対外援助法案に対して，力強く前向きの行動をとるべきです。懸案の政府支出金についての法案に対しても同様の行動をとるべきなのです。

　これらの行動を起こそうとする精神の芽ばえの中で，議会は行政部門の全面的な協力と支持が期待できます。特に政府はお金を使う場合はできる限り倹約，節約して使います，と約束します。政府はお金を使っただけの価値があることをします。政府はよく考えて行動しているという見本と節約してやりくりをしているという見本をお見せします。このことは十分に満たされていない要求を満たさない，というのでも約束を守らないというのでもありません。われわれは両方やるのです。

　両議院に長く仕えた一人として，立法部門は独立し，他からの圧力に屈してはいけないと強く信じております。そしてこのことをいつまでも尊重していきます。このことは私の骨の髄まで浸透しています。と同時に議会は，わが国の特徴として意見はいつまでも対立するのですが，にもかかわらず必

the divisions of opinion which characterize our nation, to act—to act wisely, to act vigorously, to act speedily when the need arises.

The need is here. The need is now. I ask your help.

We meet in grief: but let us also meet in renewed dedication and renewed vigor. Let us meet in action, in tolerance, and in mutual understanding.

John Kennedy's death commands what his life conveyed—that America must move forward. The time has come for Americans of all races and creeds and political beliefs to understand and to respect one another. So let us put an end to the teaching and preaching of hate and evil and violence. Let us turn away from the fanatics of the far left and the far right, from the apostles of bitterness and bigotry, from those defiant of law, and those who pour venom into our nation's bloodstream.

I profoundly hope that the tragedy and the torment of these terrible days will bind us together in new fellowship, making us one people in our hour of sorrow. So let us here highly resolve that John Fitzgerald Kennedy did not live—or die—in vain. And on this Thanksgiving eve, as we gather together to ask the Lord's blessing, and give Him our thanks, let us unite in those familiar and cherished words:

"America, America,

要なときには分別を持って，強制的に，即座に議決する能力と資格を持っていると強く信じています。

　その必要性が今，ここにあるのです。皆さんの御協力をお願いします。

　われわれは今，悲しみの中にいます。しかし新たな献身と新たな活気を生み出しましょう。行動に移しましょう。寛大になりましょう。お互い理解しましょう。

　ケネディ大統領がなくなった今，われわれは彼が生涯をかけて残してくれたことを引き継ぐわけです。つまりアメリカは前進しなくてはなりません。アメリカ人が人種によらず，信条によらず，政治的信念によらずお互いに理解し合い，尊敬し合うときがやってきました。憎しみ合うことや，悪事を働くことや，暴力で解決することを教えたり主張するのはもう止めにしましょう。極右主義者や極左主義者，反感をもち，偏狭な信条を持った使者や，法を破る人やわが国の血流に毒を注ぐようなことをする人の言うことは聞かないようにしましょう。

　最近，苦しく悲しい日々が続きますが，この悲しみの中でこそわれわれに新しい仲間意識が芽ばえ，一致協力するようになり，一国民として団結するのではないかと心から願っております。だから，ここで大いに決意しましょう。ケネディ大統領が在職中にやってくれたことと，故ケネディ大統領の死をむだにしないと。この感謝祭前夜に，主の御加護がありますようにそして神に感謝を捧げようと皆で集まっているのですから，皆さんよく御存知のこの歌を歌いましょう。
　　　　　アメリカよアメリカよ

God shed His grace on thee,
And crown thy good
With brotherhood
From sea to shining sea."

神が汝の上に恵みを垂れ給わんことを
すべての同胞の友愛を
汝の美徳の頂きに置き給わんことを

NOTES

INAUGURAL ADDRESS
（就 任 演 説）

　ケネディ前大統領は1961年1月20日に正式に米国第35代の大統領の地位に就任した。当日おこなわれた彼の就任演説は，想を練り文をみがくこと30回と伝えられ，簡潔な表現と格調の高さにおいて，リンカーン，ウィルソン，ルーズベルト等の就任演説に匹敵する歴史的名演説といわれている。

Page Line
- 2　2　**not a victory of party**　「党の勝利を祝っているのではない」という意味。ケネディ大統領が所属していた民主党の勝利を祝うという面をおさえて全国民の代表——大統領——として自由の祭典，すなわち就任式を祝うことが強調されている。
- 　　5-6　**the same solemn oath**　今から約175年前の1787年に憲法によって制定された宣誓。アメリカの大統領は就任式で次のような宣誓を行なう。

> "I do solemnly swear (affirm) that I will faithfully execute the Office of President of the United States, and will to the best of my ability, preserve, protect and defend the Constitution of the United States."

- 　　8-9　**man holds in his mortal hands**　「神ならぬ人間の手にゆだねる」
- 　　11　**the same revolutionary beliefs**　「同じ革命的信念」アメリカの革命的信念は1776年に発表された「独立宣言」の次の一文によく示されている。

> "We hold these truths to be self-evident, that all men are created equal, that they are endowed by their Creator with certain unalienable Rights, that among

NOTES

these are Life, Liberty and the pursuit of Happiness."

4　6　**we shall pay any price**　「われわれはいかなる代価をも支払うであろう」未来における強い決意をあらわすために"shall"を用いた。このあとにもこれと同じ"we shall"が出てくる。英語の伝統に従って will と shall の使い分けをしていることも，この演説を荘重にしている。

12-3　**"United, there is little ... Divided, there is little ..."**　簡潔な対句になっていてきわめて効果的である。なお，この"divided"は新約聖書マタイ伝12章25節の有名な"house ... divided against itself shall not stand."（分裂した家は立つことは出きない）からの引用である。ちなみに，この句はリンカーンの演説にも引用されている。

24　**by riding the back of the tiger ...**「虎にまたがって権力をえようとしたものは，結局虎にくわれてしまった」の意味。これは作者不明のつぎの limerick（俗謡）からとったものである。

　　There was a young lady of Niger
　　Who smiled as she rode on a tiger,
　　They returned from the ride
　　With the lady inside
　　And a smile on the face of the tiger.

6　6　**our sister republics south of our border**　中南米20の共和国をさしている。これらの国はアメリカ合衆国と目下OAS（米州機構）を結成している。この米州機構は1948年ボゴタで開かれた第9回米州会議において発足したもので，単なる軍卓同盟ではなく，経済的，社会的，文化的な協力機構である。

18　**our last best hope**　前述のthe United Nations と同格。この言葉は1862年12月1日のリンカーンの議会への教書からの引用である。すなわち "We shall nobly save, or meanly lose, *the last, best hope*, on earth."

23　**its writ may run**　writ は文書，つまり国際憲章のことをさす。「国連憲章のおよぶ限り」

8　21-2　**the absolute power to destroy other nations**「他国家を破壊する絶対的な力」，すなわち，原子兵器のこと。

10　1-2　**"undo the heavy burdens ..."**「くびきのひもをとき ...しいたげられたる者を放ち去らせ」旧約聖書イザヤ書第

58章6節からの引用。
- 8–9 **the first one hundreds days**　「初めの百日間」ルーズベルト大統領が1933年3月4日就任と同時に最悪の事態にあった恐慌を克服するために特別議会を召集し，6月14日の閉会までの約百日間にニューディール政策を特徴づける14の重要法案を成立させた。歴史家はこのことを重要視してニューディールの「最初の百日間」と称している。
- 10 **in the life of this Administration**　「この政権の任期の間に」
- 13 **In your hands ...**　リンカーンの第一就任演説のつぎの言葉と比較して頂きたい。

　　In your hands, my dissatisfied fellow-country-men, and not in mine, is the momentous issue of civil war ..."
- 22 **a long twilight struggle**　「長い夜あけ前の戦い」
- 23 **"rejoicing in hope, patient in tribulation"**　「望みをいだいて喜び，艱難に耐え」新約聖書ローマ人への手紙第12章12節からの引用。

12　13 **ask not**　「～を求めてはならない」do not ask が現代英語。この形は欽定聖書や Shakespeare によく出てくる。演説を荘重にするためにリンカーンやチャーチルも同じような使い方をしている。
- 23 **with history the final judge of our deeds, let us ...**　「われわれの行為の最後の審判者である歴史とともに」この最後の言葉はリンカーンの第二就任演説の有名な結末と構文がよく似ている。

　　With malice toward none; *with* charity for all; with firmness in the right, as God give us to see the light, *let us* strive on to finish the work *we* are in ...

THE STRATEGY OF PEACE
（平和の戦略）

　故ケネディ大統領の演説のなかでも最も重要なものの一つで，1963年6月10日，ワシントン市にあるアメリカン大学の卒業式に臨んで行なわれたものである。米国の平和戦略を説くと共にソ連に対する米国の態度を再検討しようではないかと示唆する名演説である。

NOTES

14　2　**John Masefield** (1878―1967) [méis-fi:ld, 米=méiz-] 英国の詩人・劇作家。1930年以来桂冠詩人。ケネディ大統領の死を悼み次のような死を献げた。

> All generous hearts lament the leader killed,
> The young chief with the smile, the radiant face,
> The winning way that turned a wonderous race
> Into sublimer pathways, treading on.
>
> Grant to us Life that though the man be gone
> The promise of his spirit be fulfilled.

　　15　**Pax Americana** [pǽks əmériká:nə] 米国が関係国に対して強制する平和。

16　12　**seed** 集合的に用いて「種子(タネ)」, つまり穀物のこと。小麦や米にはストロンチウム (Sr 90), セシウム (Cr 130) のような放射性物質が含まれる。

　　19　**much less the most efficient** 「いうまでもなく最も有効な方法ではない」前にある not と結合して, 否定を強調する意味となる。

18　8　**help bring** help が不定形動詞 bring を伴うことに注意。

　　27-1　**fantasies** 「幻想」の意であるが, 次に fanatics 「狂信者」が出てくるから, 「空想家」と訳せばよい。

22　23-4　**"The wicked flee when no man pursueth."** 「誰にも追跡されずとも, 悪者は逃亡する」出典は旧約聖書箴言（ソロモンのことわざ）第28章の１。

24　24　**industrial base** 工業基地または工業地帯。

26　14　**counter-weapons** 「対抗兵器」特に核兵器に対するもの。

28　8-9　**pointing the finger of judgment** 「審判の指を指し示す」とは, 批判を下すの意。

　　24　**collective death-wish** 「集団的な死滅を願うこと」つまり, 核戦争による人類の滅亡を意味している。

30　24　**West New Guinea** [njù:-gíni] West Irian 「西イリン」のこと。New Guinea 島の西半分を占める地域。1949年以来その帰属をめぐってオランダとインドネシアとの間に紛争が続いていたが, 国連及びアメリカその他のあっせんで解決し, 1963年5月, インドネシア領となった。

34　4-5　**a direct line between Moscow and Washington** ワシ

NOTES 125

ントンとモスクワを連絡する直通テレタイプ回線。米ソ両国政府の連絡を密接にするため1963年8月31日に開通した。

26 **a treaty to outlaw nuclear tests**　「核実験を禁止する条約」この演説の45日後——1963年7月25日にモスクワで部分的核実験停止条約交渉が妥結した。Banning Nuclear Tests の演説を参照。

38　7 **Peace Corps**　「平和部隊」世界の低開発国に米国の青年を送り，国際的視野を広げさせると共に，技術教育などによって現地の開発に寄与する計画。隊員は現地国民と同じ水準の生活をし，英語教育・農業技術・公衆衛生などの指導にあたる。1961年3月1日に発足し，毎年500人乃至1,000人の隊員が海外に派遣されている。

8 **National Service Corps**　「国民奉仕隊」上記にある平和部隊の国内計画としてケネディ大統領が実施を提唱していた。いずれ正式に発足するものと思われる。

13–4 **the peace is not secure because freedom is incomplete**　「自由が不完全なために平和が確立していない」とは，黒人に対する偏見から南部地方におこった暴動のことを言っている。

15 **Executive Branch**　「行政府」アメリカの政治は三権分立で大統領を中心とする Executive Branch，法律を制定する議会 Legislative Branch（立法府），及び，最高裁を中心とする Judicial Power（司法権）の三つの権力が併立している。

24–7 **"When a man's ways ... to be at peace with him."**　「人の道が主を喜ばせる時，主はその人の敵をもその人と和らがせられる」旧約聖書箴言第16章第7節からの引用であるが，米国とソ連の関係を示す意味で引用したものと考えられる。

BANNING NUCLEAR TESTS
（核実験停止条約に関する演説）

　大気圏内，大気圏外および水中における核兵器実験を禁止する条約についての米，英，ソ三国の交渉がモスクワで妥結した翌日，1963年7月26日にアメリカ国民に対してなされた放送演説の全文である。故ケネディ大統領がこの部分的核停条約を基礎として地下実験をも禁止

する全面的核実験停止条約の妥結のために努力しようとしていたことが示されている。

44　1　**Yesterday**　この演説が放送された前日—1963年7月25日—三国核実験停止条約調印の交渉がモスクワで妥結した。この歴史的な条約は8月5日，モスクワでアメリカのラスク国務長官，英国のヒューム外相，ソ連のグロムイコ外相によって調印された。

　　2–4　**a treaty to ban all nuclear tests in the atmosphere, in outer space and underwater**　「大気圏内，大気圏外および水中における核兵器実験を禁止する条約」

　　7　**Bernard Baruch**　[bəːnáːd bərùːk]　バルーク（1870—1965）米国の財政家・政治家。1946年6月6日，国連原子力委員会第一回会議で，彼が発表した原子力国際管理に関する米国の提案は，バルーク案（Baruch plan）として知られている。国際原子力開発機関の創設，原子力兵器の製造禁止，原子力の平和利用などの実現に努力すべきことが提案されている。

　　12　**international inspection**　「国際査察」
　　13　**on-the-spot inspection**　「現状査察」
　　19–20　**limited treaty**　「部分的条約」
　　22　**control posts**　監規所

46　14　**unilateral moratorium**　「一方的な核実験停止」moratoriumは，一般的に法律による支払停止または延期を意味しているが，ここでは核実験の停止の意味に使われている。

48　11　**This treaty is not the millennium**　「本条約は絶対平和の到来を意味するものではない」millennium [miléniəm] は新約聖書黙示録20章1〜7にある言葉で，至福千年期，すなわち，キリストが再臨して，この地上に幸福な状態が千年間続くという意味。ここでは「絶対平和」とでも訳せばよい。

50　16–7　**Nuclear test ban negotiations**「核実験停止交渉」核実験停止条約調印を目的とする会議は1958年7〜8月に専門家会議がジュネーブで開かれ，続いて同年10月31日から米英ソ3国の核停会議が同地で開かれた。この会議は難航を重ね，61年9月，ソ連の核実験再開につづき米英も再開，61年1月29日，3年3ヵ月，353回にわたったジュネーブ核実験停止会議は決裂状態で終った。その後，1963年2月12日に開かれたジュネーブの18ヵ国軍縮委員会の本会議で核停討議が再開され，続いて会議の舞台がモスクワに移り，今回の妥結が成

		立した。
54	1	**"would envy the dead"** 「死んだ者をうらやましがるだろう」フルシチョフ首相が中共に対してした警告をそのまま引用しているので quotation mark になっている。
56	18	**four current nuclear powers** 米・英・ソ・仏の4国が，核兵器を現在所有している。
58	6	**accidental war** 「偶発戦争」偶然や誤算による戦争。最近，アメリカでベストセラーになった小説 *Fail Safe* は偶発戦争のおそろしさを描いている。
60	25	**megaton** [mégetʌn] 1メガトンは100万トン。TNT（高性能爆薬）100万トンに相当する爆発力で水爆について使う単位。
66	8–9	**they have no lobby here in Washington** ここの they は children や grandchildren を指す。lobby は議会のロビーで議員に陳情・嘆願などをする院外団。It is 以下全文は，この条約は，特に，議会に陳情団体を持たない子孫のためのものであるという意味。
68	1	**The familiar contest between choice and coercion** 「選択と強制の間の相変わらずの抗争」この句は次の the familiar places of danger and conflict「相変わらず危険と紛争に満ちた場所」と対句になっている。
	17–8	**"A journey of a thousand miles must begin with a single step"** 「千里の道も一歩から」老子第64章に「千里行始於足下」とある。

BUILDING THE PEACE
（平和の建設）

1963年9月20日，国連総会における演説で，世界の緊張を緩和し，積極的な平和建設を説く印象に強く残る名演説。

70	8–9	**The mandate of the U.N. in the Congo** コンゴが独立後内紛のため混乱したのにたいし，国連が軍隊を派遣して事態収拾にあたったことをさす。
	9	**under fire** = under criticism or attack 「非難，攻撃を受ける」
	11	**The doctrine of Troika** 総長3人制のトロイカ方式。国連の総長の職を東・西・中立から選ばれた各代表の三人で分

つべきだとするソ連の提案。

72　5　**U.N. Decade of Development**　「国連開発の10年」低開発国を発展させるため，第16回国連総会は1960年代を開発の10年と指定した。

　　15-6　**on next Tuesday morning**　1963年9月24日火曜日，アメリカの上院（Senate）は，部分核停条約を80対19で批准可決した。

74　10　**millennium**　ここでは，「理想的な時代」の意味に訳せばよい。（p.126）の注を参照。

78　21　**self-determination**　「自決権」「民族自決主義」アメリカの自決権に対する考え方は，ウィルソン大統領の有名なFourteen pointsによく示されている。a strict observance of the principle that in determining all such questions of sovereignty, the interests of the populations concerned must have equal weight with the equitable claims of the government whose title is to be determined.

80　23-4　**emergency communications link between our capitals**　ワシントン・モスクワ間を直接連絡する直通テレタイプ回線のこと。

82　8　**war by accident or miscalculation**　「偶然や誤算による戦争」つまり，機械的故障のためとか，相手側の戦力を過小評価したためにしかけられる戦争。Banning Nuclear Testsの演説（p.58）及び（p.127）の注を参照。

　　15-6　**with adequate inspection and enforcement**　「適切な査察と協定実施制度を伴った」これは，ジュネーブで開かれていた核停会議でアメリカが常に要求してきた点である。

84　5　**engines of war**　「戦争の道具」つまり核兵器・軍用機・軍艦などの意。institutions of peace の対比語として使われている。

86　7　**make an agreement at their expense**　同盟国（their は allies の意）を犠牲にしてまでもソ連と協定を結ばない。

　　10　**"bury"**　フルシチョフ首相が，アメリカに対して "We will bury you." と言った言葉を，故ケネディ大統領が逆に引用している。

　　25-1　**plunder and pollution**　「資源の強奪や環境の汚染」つまり，自然の環境を工業や放射性物質によって浸蝕し，汚染すること。

NOTES

88	27	**U.N. conference on trade**「国連貿易開発会議」経済社会理事会が1964年3月24日から12週間の会期で召集した。
90	8	**World Health Organization**「世界保健機構」1948年発足。WHOとして知られている。事務局はジュネーブにあり，国際衛生条約の改正，医薬品の国際的標準化，疫病に対する各国の援助などを主な任務としている。日本は1951年5月に加入した。
	19	**wild game preserves** 「禁猟区」
	26	**"Food for peace" program** 「平和のための食糧計画」アイゼンハワー元大統領が，1959年1月29日に発表した教書で提案し実施にうつされたもので，主要な食糧生産国が不足国に提供する計画。
94	8	**apartheid** [əpáːthaid]「人類隔離政策」特に南アフリカで計画された非白人種差別政策のこと。
96	10	**Malaysia** [məléiʃə] マラヤ，シンガポール，北ボルネオ，サラワクが合併し，1963年9月16日に独立した連邦共和国。
	16	**failing to meet their own** 最後に obligation を補って訳せばよい。ソ連とその他共産諸国が国連軍コンゴ派遣費などの分担を拒否していることをさす。
98	5–8	**"no man who puts his hand to the plow ... kingdom of God."**「手をすきにかけてから，うしろを見る者は，神の国にふさわしくないものである。」ルカ伝9章62節からの引用。
100	2–3	**conventions of peace**「平和協定（または規約）」agreements を使わないで conventions を使ったのは，inventions of war（戦争のための発明）と rhyme させるためであろう。
	24	**Archimedes** [áːrkimiːdíːz] アルキメデス（287–212 BC）ギリシャの数学者・物理学者。「アルキメデスの原理」を発見した。
	25	**principle of the lever** 「テコの原理」
102	1–2	**"Give me a place where I can stand—and I shall move the world."**「私が立っていられる足場を与えてくれないか，そうすれば世界を動かして見せよう。」

WE WILL CARRY ON
（続けようではありませんか）

ジョンソン米大統領の議会演説

　リンドン・B・ジョンソン第36代米大統領は，1963年11月27日，アメリカ議会上下両院の合同会議において，就任後最初の演説を行なった。この中で新大統領は，故ケネディ大統領の残した業績を引きついでいく決意を明らかにし，米国民に向ってこの歩みを「続けようではないか」という呼びかけを行なった。

104　3-4　**All I have I would have given gladly not to be standing here today.** "would have given" は勿論仮定法。このセンテンスは日本語に直訳するよりも次のように意訳した方がよい。「今日，この壇上に立つにあたって，まことに万感胸に迫る思いをするのであります。」

　　13-4　**the forward thrust of America**「アメリカの力強い前進」

106　22　**match national strength with national restraint**　「国家の力と国家の自制力とを釣り合わせる」

108　20-1　**For thirty-two years, Capitol Hill has been my home.**「この32年間，連邦議事堂は私にとっていわばわが家であった。」ジョンソン大統領は1931年テキサス州選出下院議員の秘書として公職の道へのスタートをきった。以来，1938年には通常任期の下院議員に選出され，連続5期にわたって下院議員を勤めた。続いて1948年には任期6年の上院議員に選出され，その5年後の1953年には44才で上院民主党院内総務になった。その後，1954年に上院議員に再選され，1960年の民主党公認副大統領に選れた。

　　20　**Capitol Hill**　国会議事堂のある地域で国会議事堂の意味にもよく使われている。

110　19　**Alliance for Progress in this hemisphere**「西半球の進歩のための同盟」故ケネディ大統領が1961年3月に提唱してつくられたもの。

　　22-5　**"in the first one thousand days, ... let us begin."** ケネディ大統領の就任演説からの引用。本書の（$p.10$：$ll.9\sim12$）参照。

112　8　**Civil Rights Bill**　「公民権法案」故ケネディ大統領は就任

NOTES

　　　以来，公民権を確立するため各種の政策と措置をとり，人種差別撤廃のため努力した。
　11　**100 years or more**　約100年前のリンカーン大統領の時代（1861〜1865）に奴隷解放宣言（Emancipation Proclamation）が発表され，アメリカにおける黒人の自由と平等が擁護された。
　21　**Tax Bill**　「税政法案」
114　6-7　**Foreigh Aid Bill**　「対外援助法案」
　22-3　**both houses of the Congress**　「議会両院」アメリカの議会は Senate（米国上院）と Lower House（下院）の二院制である。
116　27　**"America, America, …"**　アメリカの愛国歌の一つとして親しまれている "America, the Beautiful" からの一節。この歌の作詞者は Katherine Lee Dates で第二次大戦後多くの人々に愛唱されるようになった。次のような意味である。
118　1　**God shed His grace on thee**　「神が汝の上に恵を垂れ給わんことを」
　2　**crown thy good**　「汝の美徳の頂に置き給わんことを」
　3　**With brotherhood**　「同胞の友愛を」
　4　**From sea to shining sea**　「海から輝ける海まで」→「アメリカすべての」

CDについて

　この対訳には，アメリカ大使館ラジオ部の御厚意によって入手した故ケネディ大統領の生前の声の記録であるテープがあります。大使館より提供された演説実況録音は延べ5時間以上にものぼるもので，特に印象に残る箇所だけを選び，一時間の教材用CDとして編集制作しました。

　実況録音のうち，就任演説のテキストは，就任式当日故ケネディ大統領の口から出たものですが，他の演説テキストは，予定原稿によっているため，録音と原稿の間にごくわずかくいちがいがあることをおことわりしておきます。

　なおCDには，1961年1月20日，就任式当日，アメリカの有名な黒人歌手，マリアン・アンダソンが独唱したアメリカ国歌と，故ケネディ大統領の「宣誓の言葉」（p. 2の注参照）の貴重な録音も収録されています。

　勿論，このテキストは，CDなしでも十分に使用できることは言うまでもありません。しかし，演説者の生（なま）の声を聞いて英語を勉強することのできるCDの長所を存分に活用されることをおすすめします。

　またCDの日本語解説の語り手には内藤和子元NHKアナウンサーにお願いしました。

（訳注者）

訳注者紹介

長谷川　潔
(は せ がわ　きよし)

1927年横浜生まれ。
南カリフォルニア大学大学院修了。
元横浜国立大学教授／元関東学院大学教授。
フルブライト・アリゾナ大学名誉教授。

主な著書
『日本語からみた英語』（サイマル出版会）
『放送による英語の聞き方学び方』（ジャパンタイムズ）
『英語放送の聞き方と発音練習』（共著、南雲堂）
など多数ある。

英和対訳ケネディ大統領演説集CD付

2007年 6 月15日　　1 刷
2024年 7 月29日　　6 刷

訳注者　　長谷川　潔
発行者　　南雲一範
発行所　　株式会社　南雲堂
　　　　　〒162-0801　東京都新宿区山吹町361
　　　　　電　話（03）3268-2384（営業部）
　　　　　　　　（03）3268-2387（編集部）
　　　　　FAX　（03）3260-5425（営業部）
　　　　　振替口座　00160-0-46863
印刷所／日本ハイコム株式会社　　製本所／松村製本所

Printed in Japan　　〈検印者略〉
乱丁、落丁本はご面倒ですが小社通販係宛ご送付下さい。
送料小社負担にてお取替えいたします。

ISBN 978-4-523-42283-9　C0082　〈A-283〉

南雲堂の **好評英語学習参考書!**
史上最高のコラボ完成!!
安河内哲也×英単語ピーナツ

センターから
やり直しまで

英語はピー単を音読しろ!

英単語ピーナツ
BASIC 1000

CD Book

安河内哲也
佐藤誠司　共著

● 英語学参・語学書
● 四六版／280ページ

ISBN978-4-523-25156-9 C7082

定価（本体 1,200 円＋税）

**英語学参のベストセラー作者が伝授する
英語で人生を切り開く方法とは！**

アドラー流
英語で幸せになる勇気

小池 直己 著

> 努力と英語は決して裏切らない。
> アドラーの教えをもとに、夢と希望をもって
> 英語の勉強を楽しみ、人生に楽しみを見出そうと
> している人は必ず幸せになれる。

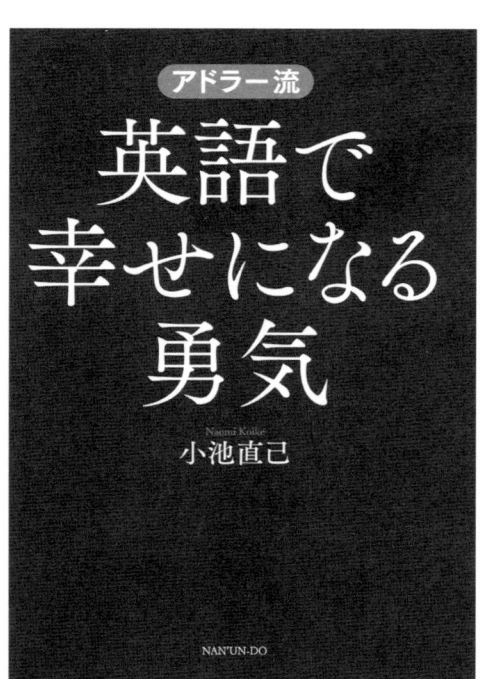

第1章～第5章：
お金を使わずに効率的に英語力を身に付ける方法

第6章～第16章：
有名英語講師としての実体験・実話を基にした逆境を前向きに生きる方法

英語が専門でなかった私がなぜ370冊もの英語学習書を書けたのか？ 英語科出身でもない私がなぜ英語教師として幸せな人生を歩んでこられたのか？ 心理学的アプローチに基づく「英語との向き合い方」と小池流「英語学習のノウハウ」をこの1冊に凝縮しました。

四六判 288ページ
定価（本体 1,500円＋税）
ISBN978-4-523-26562-7　C0082

南雲堂
〒162-0801 東京都新宿区山吹町361
e-mail: nanundo@post.email.ne.jp
TEL: 03-3268-2384
FAX: 03-3260-5425

大学英語テキストで大ヒットを飛ばし続ける教材開発のカリスマ、A・ベネット氏渾身の2冊！

アンドル・ベネット著
A5判　288ページ 定価(本体1,500円+税)

ベネット先生の
イラスト付き
語源で一気にマスター英単語
＜接頭辞・接尾辞まとめ編＞

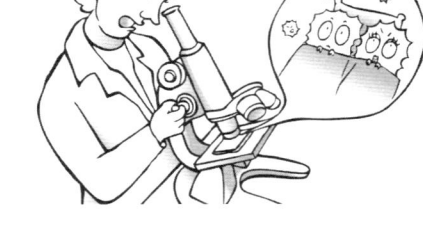

アンドル・ベネット著
A5判　256ページ 定価(本体1,400円+税)

ベネット先生の
イラスト付き
語源で一気にマスター英単語
＜語根まとめ編＞

● 音声フリーダウンロード付き ●

- ◉ 単語学習効果に定評のある語源中心の英単語集です。
- ◉ 学習効率向上のためのイラストを効果的に配置！
- ◉ 実績のあるネイティブによる例文の提示！
- ◉ 学習に便利な赤色暗記シート付き！

南雲堂